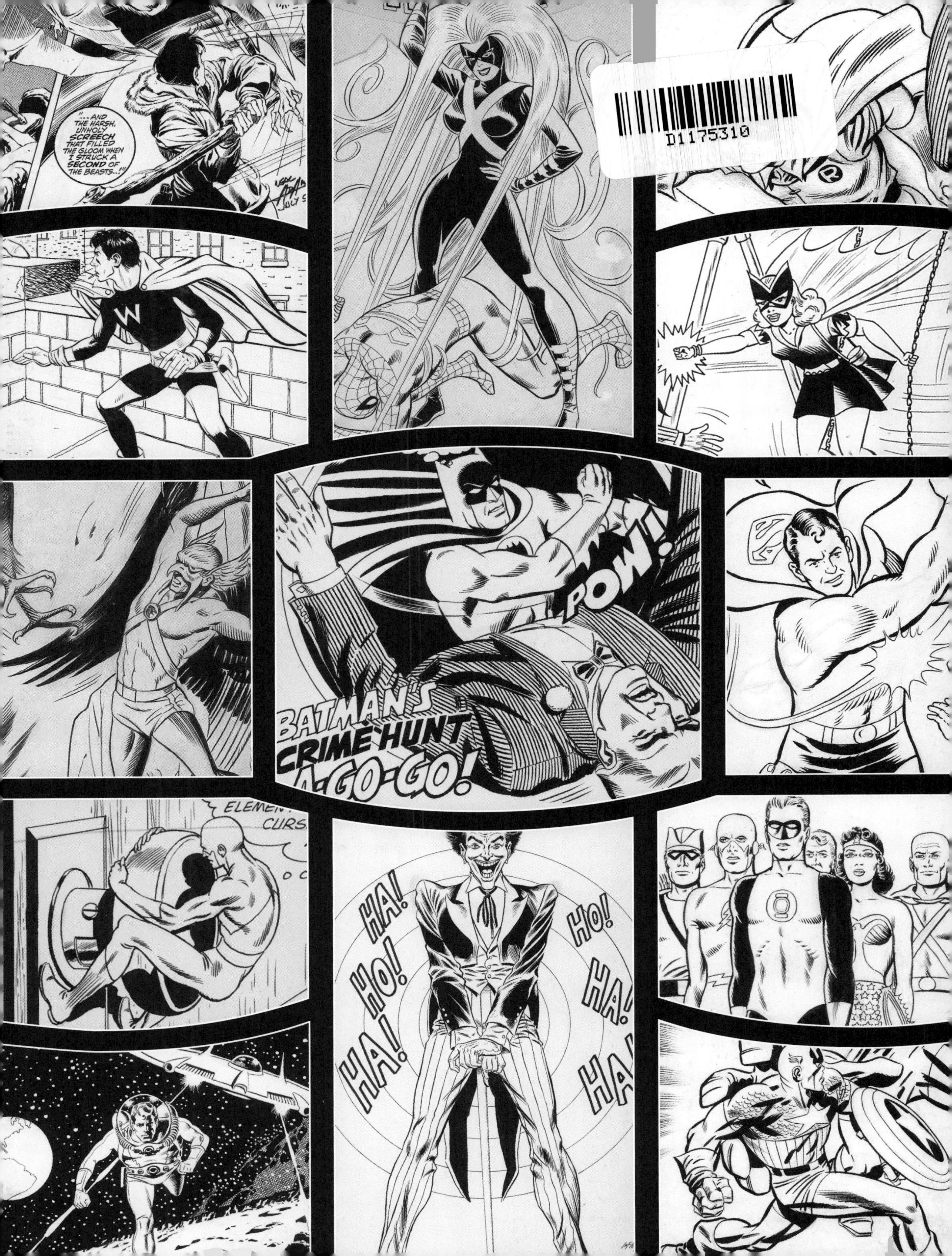

"...AND THE HARSH, UNHOLY SCREECH THAT FILLED THE GLOOM WHEN I STRUCK A SECOND OF THE BEASTS...!"
POW!
BATMAN'S CRIME HUNT A-GO-GO!
HA!
HO!
HO!
HA!
HO!
HA!
HA!

RISE OF THE SUPERHEROES

GREATEST SILVER AGE COMIC BOOKS AND CHARACTERS

DAVID W. TOSH

Published by

Krause Publications, a division of F+W Media, Inc.
700 East State Street • Iola, WI 54990-0001
715-445-2214 • 888-457-2873
www.krausebooks.com

To order books or other products call toll-free 1-800-258-0929
or visit us online at www.krausebooks.com

ISBN-13: 9781440248160
ISBN-10: 1440248168

Designed by Rebecca Vogel
Edited by Kristine Manty

Printed in China

10 9 8 7 6 5 4 3 2 1

CONTENTS

INTRODUCTION

IT'S NO secret that our society today is obsessed with super-powered heroes in colorful costumes. All you need to do is take a look at the movies that have been popular over the past few years. Superman, Batman, Captain America, Spider-Man, the Suicide Squad, Deadpool, the Avengers — all have been money-makers at the box office. The small screen also has been loaded with superheroes like Supergirl, Daredevil, The Flash, Agent of SHIELD; these, and many more, are being faithfully followed by millions each week.

Why are these characters so popular? When did comic book superheroes become so big in America's popular culture?

For me, this story goes back many years, to the summer I turned eight. It was a Sunday afternoon, after church. Mom, Dad and I had just finished our lunch when he decided to go to the big newsstand in downtown Houston. I liked books at that young age, and was especially fond of newspaper comic strips like *Dennis the Menace*, but comic books weren't the kind of thing I had much exposure to. My grandmother kept a tattered stack of them for my older cousins during family visits, and I had glanced at one or two without thinking much

about them. I was, however, fond of the television series, *The Adventures of Superman*, which was being shown at the time in reruns every weekday afternoon. I had recently overheard a

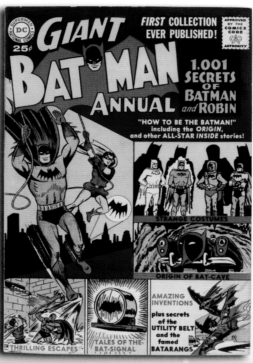

The one that got me hooked!

couple of kids discussing Superman, and I guess it got me curious. The newsstand had a big selection of them toward the back of the store, and I found myself gravitating in their direction. And what a colorful display all those comic covers offered! In those days before Marvel made a lasting impact, DC was the big name in the business, and I loved looking over all these mysterious covers with titles like *Action*, *The Brave and the Bold*, *Adventure*, and *Challengers of the Unknown*. I was permitted to pick out one

comic, but instead of Superman, I wound up grabbing the comic that would change my life going forward — a copy of the very first *Batman Annual*. I was hooked from that moment on!

Superhuman characters have piqued the public's imagination since the earliest stories and myths passed down from generation to generation. From biblical heroes like Samson and David, to Hercules and Greek gods, to more contemporary legends like Paul Bunyan and John Henry, these larger-than-life myths were a part of our culture. In the 1920s, adventure comic strips began appearing in the papers, filled with the exploits of "supermen" like Captain Easy, Buck Rogers, Flash Gordon, and Tarzan (who made the leap from pulp fiction to comics, and then movies). Little wonder then, that Superman made such a big impression when *Action Comics* #1, cover-dated July 1938, first went on sale. The late 1930s through to the end of World War II in 1945 saw many colorfully costumed crimefighters competing for kid's dimes, but as the war ended, most of these muscle-bound mysterymen began to lose favor with readers. Even one of the biggest selling supermen of all time had finally run his course by 1953, when the original Captain Marvel ceased publication. Lurid crime and horror comics became all the rage, along with Westerns, teen humor, romance, war, and science fiction, plus satirical humor in titles like *MAD*, *Get Lost*, and *Flip*, were big with kids.

But on the horizon came a new era for the supermen (and women), and it all began in 1956. By the 1960s, caped crusaders ruled the newsstands once again, this time bigger than ever — and I was there to take it all in. It was a wonderful time to be a kid!

This book is a personal recollection of those halcyon years that collectors refer to as the Silver Age of Comics. To me, this was the medium's finest time, and the very best time to be a fan. I'm sure every dedicated comics fan thinks of his or her earliest exposure to the form as being the best, and there have certainly been great comics in just about every era, but for me, the superheroes of the swinging sixties were simply unbeatable. They were tailor-made for the era, guaranteed to make these throwaway children's publications rise above all expectations and become as important an art form as anything produced by artists held in the highest esteem by the general public. Let's all take a look back at "those thrilling days of yesteryear," as they used to say on old-time radio. It'll be a fun trip, I assure you!

Special note: Unless otherwise noted in the captions, all photos featured in this book are courtesy of Heritage Auction's archives.

Marvel Studios/Walt Disney Studios Motion Pictures

DC Films/Warner Bros. Pictures

Wonder Woman and The Avengers have a lasting legacy in modern pop culture, and movies starring these characters have earned millions, even billions, of dollars at the box office domestically. Wonder Woman's first solo outing in 2017's self-titled film was a huge blockbuster, earning more than $412.5 million domestically. The Avengers' franchise has earned $1.1 billion domestically.

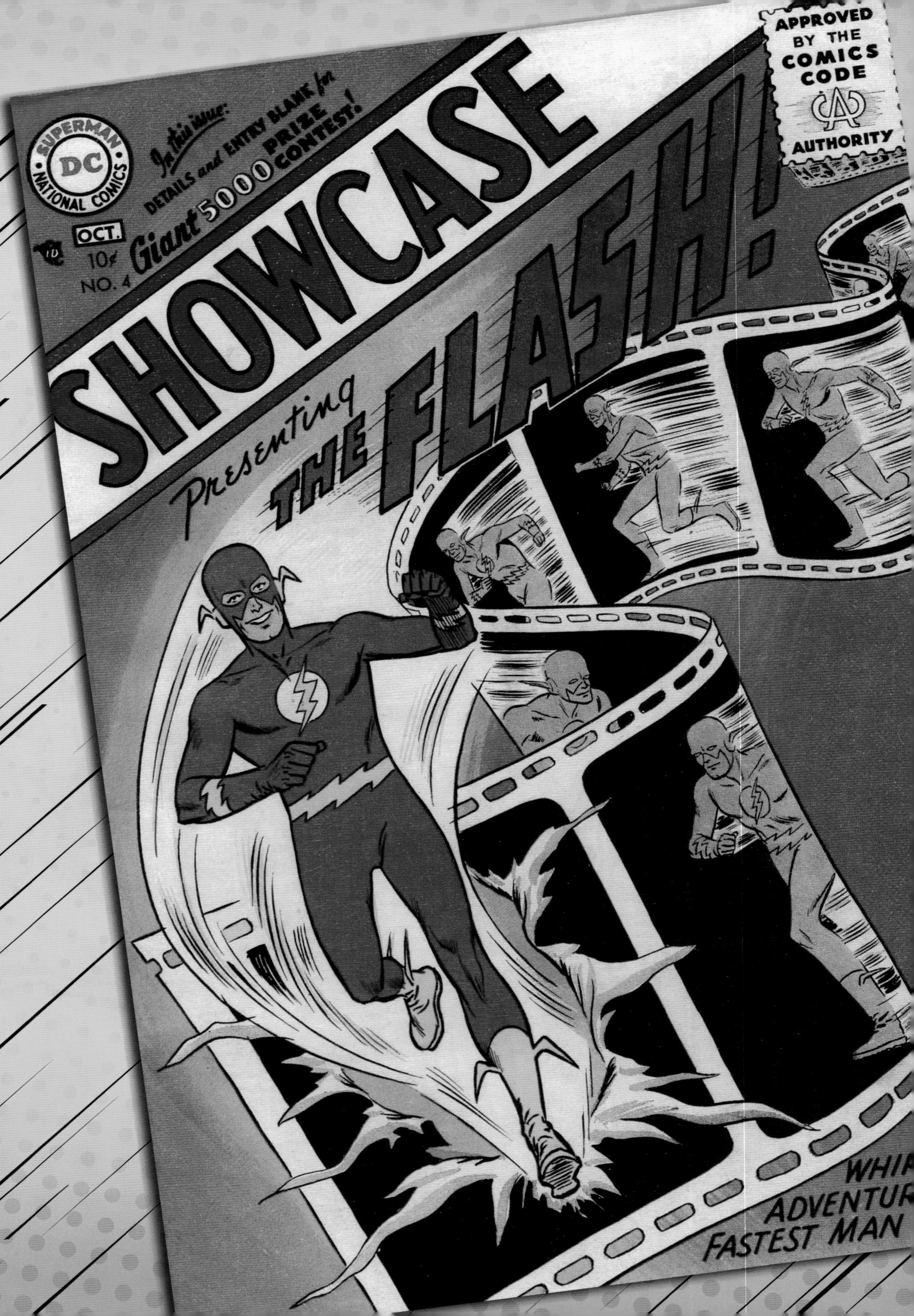
APPROVED BY THE COMICS CODE AUTHORITY
SUPERMAN DC NATIONAL COMICS
OCT.
10¢
NO. 4
In this issue:
DETAILS and ENTRY BLANK for
Giant 5000 PRIZE CONTEST!
SHOWCASE
Presenting
THE FLASH!
WHI
ADVENTU
FASTEST MAN

CHAPTER 1

OLD STANDBYS
AND
NEW BEGINNINGS

COSTUMED SUPERHEROES in comic books had been popular during World War II, but by 1946, their popularity began to slip. By 1950, many of the old guard had been retired, and for some of those that remained, the clock was definitely ticking. The original Captain Marvel had been one of (if not the) biggest selling superhero comic book during the forties, but a long-simmering lawsuit with DC over the similarities between the "Big Red Cheese" and Superman finally ended in 1953, effectively finishing the series.

Marvel's "Timely" imprint was shifting gears in its publications, pushing its remaining heroic characters in different directions — horror for Captain America, fighting communist enemies instead of garden-variety criminals for the Human Torch and Sub-Mariner. Over at Fox, their standard torch-bearer, the Blue Beetle, had wound down his heroic exploits around 1950, not to resurface again until 1955 for a short, unsuccessful run with Charlton. Quality Comics sold out to DC after dumping most of its superheroes in favor of detectives and soldiers.

In fact, the whole concept of brightly colored "mystery men" in comic books was rapidly replaced with crime comics that focused more on the criminals than the lawmen who always brought them in (or did away with them) by each story's end. The violence and bloodshed in these new titles like *Crime Does Not Pay* (with the word "Crime" in much larger letters than the rest of the title) led to even more gruesome comics with "horror" and "terror" being the hot-button terms to splash across the covers. Each year saw the envelope pushed further, with companies like EC and Harvey leading the blood-soaked trail. Nothing seemed to be off-limits, with sex and drugs creeping into stories. In time, parents, teachers, and clergymen demanded a change in the way their children's entertainment was presented.

Enter the Comics Code.

The 1950s saw a growing rise in juvenile delinquency. The

APPROVED
BY THE
COMICS
CODE
AUTHORITY

By 1956, with the exception of "wholesome" comic books published by Gilberton (Classics Illustrated) and Dell, all newsstand comics carried this symbol in the upper right corner of the front cover.

OPPOSITE PAGE: The first Silver Age appearance of The Flash (DC, 10/56). This "raw" (uncertified) copy in restored Fine 6.0 condition sold for $1,725 in 2009.

post-war generation was considered "lazy, spoilt, lacking in discipline, disrespectful of authority and violent." (Cliomuse.com, "Blackboard Jungle and Juvenile Delinquency in the 1950s.") Parents and teachers looked for anything to pin the blame on (certainly not the way they brought up/taught their children, of course), and youth culture's habits were picked apart and examined by the adults, looking for that scapegoat. Comic books, long-hated by many educators and child psychiatrists, were an easy target, especially the over-the-top horror titles that were popular at the time. Anxiety over the Cold War with Russia and the movie *Blackboard Jungle*, which opened with a loud bang courtesy of Bill Hailey and the Comets' "Rock Around the Clock" (the new rock and roll fad was "part of the problem" as well) pretty much sealed the deal. Something had to be done, and it was — the formation of the Comics Code Authority to curb those nasty ten centers that were corrupting the nation's children. Never mind the fact that the rise of juvenile delinquency echoed the rise in the nation's population; for these moralistic do-gooders, it simply *had* to be comic books.

The companies publishing comic books,

for the most part, had internal guidelines for what was allowed and what wasn't; even EC, the most obvious and flagrant company guilty of putting blood-dripping murder and horror stories in kid's hands, had adopted a code, displayed with a star logo on the cover that read, in part, "Conforms to the Comics Code" on all titles up to 1952. No matter, EC was the main target of the new watchdogs, and no amount of conforming would keep their ten-cent comic books on the nation's newsstands.

Some companies were a safer bet in those paranoid times. Classics Illustrated and Dell Comics ignored the code completely and were left alone, as they published what were considered wholesome, safe children's entertainment. DC had to tone down a few things, but was for the most part free to continue publishing their various titles.

THE OLD STANDBYS: SUPERMAN, BATMAN, AND WONDER WOMAN

The Man of Steel withstood the great Superhero Exodus at DC with little trouble.

Superman had been appearing in all sorts of places — newspaper comic strips, radio, movie serials, and lots of toy products for years — and had become as recognizable a cultural icon as Mickey Mouse. His comic book exploits continued uninterrupted in monthly issues of *Action Comics* and the eight-times-a-year *Superman* solo book. *The Adventures of Superman* syndicated television series starring George Reeves which has begun airing in 1952 remained popular in 1956, and continued to be aired in reruns for many years to come.

The clean-cut, good-vs-evil comic book storylines felt little effect from the new Comics Code Authority rules and regulations that put more than a few titles out of business. Superman's earlier career as a teen-aged boy also flourished in the pages of *Adventure Comics* and *Superboy*.

If anything, the Superman brand was stronger than ever, even branching out with two new titles: *Superman's Pal Jimmy Olsen*, with stories revolving around the Daily Planet cub reporter, which began in 1954, was the first. Superman appeared on every cover, and was featured to some extent in every story, with attractive artwork by Curt Swan on most of Jimmy's adventures. After a two-issue tryout in

Showcase, the suggestively titled *Superman's Girl Friend Lois Lane* began in 1958, starring Clark Kent's fellow Daily Planet reporter, Lois. Miss Lane would often rival Clark for the big stories, while unashamedly chasing after Superman with romance and marriage as her objectives. Both of these spin-off titles would run for the next twenty or so years. Superman also teamed with fellow crimebuster Batman for a series of stories running in *World's Finest Comics*. This title had begun in the early 1940s as a 96-page anthology comic with separate stories for each hero, but by issue #71, cover-dated July 1954, the two characters (plus Batman's sidekick Robin) were featured working together.

The mid-1950s saw a big rise in popularity for science-fiction films. Naturally, Superman, referred to in the TV series opening as a "strange visitor from another planet," fit right in.

Other strange visitors, including a good number of weird monster-like creatures from outer space started to appear, especially in the *World's Finest* stories drawn by Dick Sprang. While these far-out themes worked with the Man of Steel, the Gotham Guardian's encounters with outer space elements was a bit of a stretch.

Three late-fifties DC comics: *Superman* #107 and *Detective Comics* #229 on the previous page, and *Wonder Woman* #88 in "raw" state (uncertified grades).

Two different versions of the Girl of Steel: The copy of *Superman* #123, left, graded FN- 5.5, sold for $956 in 2016; the copy of *Action Comics* #252, graded VG+ 4.5, sold for $276 in 2006.

Batman had no super powers, but was no less a popular "super" hero throughout the Golden Age 1940s, in the pages of *Detective Comics* and *Batman*. As the craze for true crime comics began to die down, so did the Caped Crusader's exploits with ordinary criminals. Fantastic characters like the Joker still appeared on a fairly regular basis, but more and more often, Batman found himself facing interplanetary menaces. I personally liked those fantastic stories, but for some fans, it must have been a turn-off. Batman was hanging on, but his popularity was definitely beginning to slip.

While Batman strayed a bit from his original premise, Wonder Woman stuck quite determinedly to hers. By 1956, she appeared only in her namesake title, having lost her spot in *Sensation Comics* after issue #106, when that anthology title switched gears, and became more of a horror-suspense book. The stories appearing in *Wonder Woman* retained the unique look and feel of her Golden Age adventures, which seemed a bit old-fashioned even back then. Original artist Harry G. Peter continued handling art chores on Wonder Woman until 1958, at which

time she finally got a much-needed makeover, by way of new artistic team Ross Andru and Mike Esposito; the new team began with issue #98. Editor Bob Kanigher revamped the book with new characters, updating some of Wonder Woman's back-story elements.

These "Big Three" DC characters would continue to survive and prosper as the new Silver Age era moved into the 1960s. Big things were in store for all of them. But they weren't the only holdovers from the Golden Age. Green Arrow and Aquaman both continued to appear in short backup stories featured in *Adventure Comics* and *World's Finest Comics*.

YOUTHFUL EXPLOITS

Superman's exploits as a youth hit a milestone with *Adventure Comics* #247 (April 1958) when the Boy of Steel met three teenaged visitors from the 30th Century: Lightning Boy (later to be known as Lightning Lad), Saturn Girl, and Cosmic Boy. This was the first appearance of the Legion of Super-Heroes. This one-off story about a group of futuristic teens with strange powers proved popular enough to warrant a second appearance in *Adventure* #267 (December 1959), and they would stick around for years to come, eventually landing their own feature in *Adventure*. We'll revisit this team in the next chapter, as the sixties were the heyday for the original, expanded Legion.

SUPERGIRL DEBUT

Meanwhile, back in Superman's world, it was decided to give him a female counterpart, also from the mythical world of Krypton, original home of Kal-El (Superman). It started with a try-out issue, *Superman* #123 (August, 1958). In this "Imaginary Story," Superman's pal Jimmy Olsen is granted three wishes from a mystical miniature Indian totem pole, and his first wish was — you guessed it — a Super-Girl, who appears on the cover, helping the Man of Steel save a train; she was blonde, with a Superman top, little red skirt, and boots.

The "real" Supergirl was introduced in *Action Comics* #252 (May 1959). This time, we are told that Superman's younger cousin, Kara Zor-El, and her family lived in Argo City, which somehow survived the explosion of Krypton by way of a large fragment of the planet expelled with a protective bubble of oxygen over the city. When the city is doomed by a meteor shower, Kara's father sends her in a rocket to earth, just as Jor-El had sent baby Kal to Earth some years earlier. The front cover shows Supergirl (in full costume) popping out of her rocket to a shocked Superman. The story appears as a back

up in *Action*, where Kara/Supergirl gets her own secret identity (as orphan Linda Lee), where she secretly operates whenever Superman needs her. She would finally be revealed to the world in *Action Comics* #285 (February 1962).

THE RETURN OF THE FLASH AND GREEN LANTERN

The gutting of the comic book industry due to the Comics Code was seen as an opportunity by DC story editor Julius "Julie" Schwartz (1915-2004). Julie had been with the company since 1944, working for DC's sister company, All-American Comics (which published *Flash Comics*), *All-American Comics* (featuring The Green Lantern and other heroes), *Wonder Woman* and *Sensation Comics*, *Green Lantern*, and *All Star Comics*, home to the Justice Society of America). Before that, he was active in science-fiction fandom, publishing, along with Mort Weisinger and Forrest J. Ackerman (remember these names), one of the first SF fanzines, *Time Traveler*, in 1932. Julie's love of science fiction factored into a decision that would set the stage for the Silver Age of comic books.

DC execs Whitney Ellsworth and Julie's fanzine friend, Mort Weisinger, were in charge of a new DC title designed to present new characters and concepts, called *Showcase*, with the first issue cover-dated March-April 1956. The first three issues starred firemen, Western adventures ("Kings of the Wild"), and naval frogmen. The fourth issue (cover-dated September-October 1956) would be turned over to Julie Schwartz, and prove to be the one to break the mold by reviving The Flash. Julie and writer Robert Kanigher totally revamped the character with a new identity, new science fiction-based origin, and a slick new costume that included a cowl and skin-tight red suit. The first story, illustrated by former Golden Age Flash artists Carmine Infantino and Joe Kubert, introduced us to scientist Barry Allen. In an inspired twist, Barry is seen reading an old issue of *Flash Comics* before an accident involving lightning hitting chemicals through an open window gave him the power of speed he had been reading about. It was a great way to tie the

Action Comics #293 panel art by Al Plastino.

First "revival" issue of *The Flash* (DC, 1959); this copy, CGC NM 9.4, sold for $38,837 in 2011.

old with the new. It proved to be a hit, and by *Showcase* #8 (cover-dated May-June 1957), he was back with a second issue. He would appear two more times (issues 13 and 14, 1958) before the decision was made to give him his own title. Fittingly, that first issue picked up numbering from the old *Flash Comics*, appearing on the stands as #105, cover-dated February-March 1959.

The success of this revived character resulted in Julie picking another one of his favorite Golden Age heroes with *Showcase* #22. This issue gave us a totally revamped Green Lantern, once again created with a strong science-fiction influence. In the first story, written by John Broome and illustrated by Gil Kane and Joe Giella, we meet test pilot Hal Jordan, who encounters Abin Sur, a dying alien who was part of an interstellar police force called the Green Lantern Corps. A special power ring and energy source (in the shape of a lantern, of course) are bestowed on Jordan, who must now carry on the Corp duties, thankfully on Earth rather than the planet Abin Sur came from, and with good reason — the villain he had been chasing, Sinestro, was now loose on Earth. The new Green Lantern had his work cut out for him.

With these two important revivals, the stage was set for one of the richest, most creative decades of American comic books – the 1960s. There would never be another one like it.

The "early" Silver Age had begun, but with the dawning of a new decade, it would flourish and grow beyond anyone's expectations. That attempt by psychiatrists, teachers, and other misguided do-gooders to banish most comic books with the Comics Code resulted in a medium more robust than ever, with superheroes leading the way. Onward to the sixties!

THE FLASH'S SUPERFAN

Someone who may love The Flash even more than the superhero's own mother is *The Big Bang Theory's* Sheldon Cooper.

Over the course of the CBS sitcom's 11 seasons, Sheldon has shown his fondness for The Flash by wearing a T-shirt with the superhero's lightning-bolt symbol emblazoned across it many times and dressing up as the character in several episodes, including "The Justice League Recombination" (season 4): Sheldon dons a Flash costume, acts like him throughout the episode, and even imagines having Flash's lightning speed to zoom to the Grand Canyon to scream his frustration with Leonard. The Flash's presence is also felt in "The Commitment Determination" (season 8): Sheldon stops in the middle of making out with Amy to ask her if he should watch the new Flash TV show. Not surprisingly, she is not amused.

It was only a matter of time before The Flash met Sheldon in person, which happens in "The Dependence Transcendence" (season 10) — well, the superhero appears in a dream, but close enough. After struggling to stay awake to finish a big project, but refusing to take any caffeine for a boost, Sheldon falls asleep and later wakes up startled to see The Flash standing in front of him. The superhero encourages him to have an energy drink,

CBS Entertainment/Warner Bros. Television/Chuck Lorre Productions

which Sheldon declines because of the caffeine, and The Flash then accuses him of being uncool and says if he wants to feel like he has superpowers to try one. When Sheldon asks if superheroes take any performance enhancers, The Flash confirms that they do, including The Hulk, who is strong because of steroids, and Batman, who gets into fights because of scotch. Because he likes doing things that famous people do, Sheldon takes The Flash's dubious advice and has an energy drink; he later ends up thinking he's addicted, after wanting another one.

POP CULTURE EVENTS, 1956-59

JANUARY 1956 . . . Elvis Presley's first hit single, "Heartbreak Hotel," is released

APRIL 1956 . . . . . Actress Grace Kelly becomes Princess Grace of Monaco

MAY 1956 . . . . . . NBC debuts Peacock logo

OCTOBER 1956 . . . Don Larsen of the New York Yankees throws a perfect game in the World Series, Game 5

MOST POPULAR TV SERIES FOR 1956 . . . . *I Love Lucy*

JANUARY 1957 . . . Humphrey Bogart dies; Wham-O introduces the Frisbee; Dwight D. Eisenhower sworn in for second term as US President

MARCH 1957 . . . . Dr. Seuss' *The Cat in the Hat* is released

OCTOBER 1957 . . . TV series *Leave it to Beaver* premieres on CBS

NOVEMBER 1957 . . The Elvis Presley film, *Jailhouse Rock*, opens

JULY 1958 . . . . . . The Hula Hoop is introduced

JANUARY 1959 . . . Alaska becomes the 49th State; Disney's *Sleeping Beauty* is released to theaters

AUGUST 1959 . . . . Miles Davis releases the classic jazz album *Kind of Blue;* Hawaii becomes the 50th State

OCTOBER 1959 . . . *The Twilight Zone* premieres on CBS

IN MY NEIGHBORHOOD

WHEN THE SILVER AGE of Comics began in 1956, I was a three-year-old toddler. It would be several years before I began to read, let alone buy comics off the racks at my local drugstore. I was read to a lot by my parents, though. In fact, I learned to read before I entered first grade by having mom and dad read the same books to me over and over, to the point that I knew what the words on each page meant. How I was able to do this is a mystery to me – back then, I thought all kids learned to read in this manner.

In addition to having books read to me, I became a fan of television from early on. *The Adventures of Superman* was a constant fixture, and I loved to run around our back yard with a towel tied around my neck, pretending to fly. The stage was set for me to become an enthusiastic comic book fan and collector in just a few years.

I did come to know some of the late 1950s output of comics by picking up used copies at several locations around my area of Houston in the early sixties. My primary source was a little grocery store within walking distance from my house, run by Mrs. Harmon. She always had a stack of old comic books on the counter, which she sold at a nickel apiece. Most of them were DC titles from 1958-60. There were a couple of other places that I would go from time to time, out with my dad; one place in particular had a table loaded down with back issues. The owner of this establishment had the habit of adding staples to the spine of every comic he sold, even if the pages were firmly in place. Even at that early age, I was a nut about condition – never folding the cover and pages back as I read, keeping my comics in neat stacks in my closet, etc. Having those extra staples was a no-no, and I restricted my purchases at this location to only a few select books.

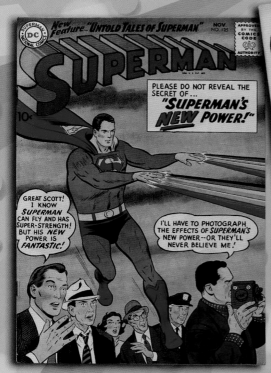

Superman #125 (DC, 11/58) CGC NM 9.4, sold for $2,868 in 2008 (then-current highest graded copy).

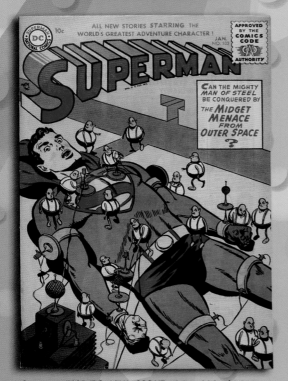

Superman #102 (DC, 1/56); CGC VF+ 8.5, sold for $1,912 in 2008.

Superman #115 (DC, 8/57); CGC NM- 9.2, sold for $2,868 (then-current highest graded copy).

Original art by Wayne Boring and Stan Kaye for *Superman* #113; sold for $8,365 in 2014.

◄ *Superman* #128 (DC, 4/59); CGC VF 8.0, sold for $191 in 2010.

ACTION COMICS
FEATURING SUPERMAN

Action Comics #234 (DC, 11/57); CGC VF/NM 9.0, sold for $507 in 2014.

Action Comics #242, first appearance of Brainiac (DC, 7/58); CGC VF- 7.5, sold for $3,734 in 2011.

▲ Action Comics #254, first meeting of Bizarro and Superman (DC, 7/59); Twin Cites pedigree copy, CGC FN/VF 7.0, sold for $262 in 2011.

◄ *Batman* #122 (DC, 3/59); CBCS VF+ 8.5, sold for $627 in 2016.

Detective Comics #233 (DC, 9/58); CGC VF 8.0, sold for $286 in 2010.

Batman #113 (DC, 2/58); CBCS FN/VF 7.0, sold for $334 in 2016.

BATMAN IN 'OUTER SPACE'

▶ *Batman* #128 (DC, 12/59), CBCS VF+ 8.5, sold for $627 in 2016.

Detective Comics #260 (DC, 10/58); CBCS VF+ 8.5, sold for $1,135 in 2016.

Detective Comics #256 (DC, 6/58); CGC VF/NM 9.0, sold for $478 in 2016.

Superman's Pal Jimmy Olsen #19 (DC, 3/57); CGC VF/NM 9.0, sold for $657 in 2008.

▲ Superman's Girl Friend Lois Lane #1 (DC, 3-4/58); CGC VF 8.0, sold for $8,962 in 2011.

Superman's Girl Friend Lois Lane #11 (DC, 8/59); CGC VF/NM 9.0, sold for $537 in 2010.

THE FLASH

The Flash #108 (DC, 8-9/59); CGC VF/NM 9.0, sold for $7,170 in 2009.

▼ Showcase #13 (DC, 3-4/58), third Silver Age appearance of The Flash; CGC NM- 9.2, sold for $13,145 in 2009.

▶ *Showcase* #22 (DC, 10/59), first Silver Age appearance of Green Lantern; CGC VF/NM 9.0, sold for $59,750 in 2009.

Showcase #23 (DC, 12/59), second Silver Age appearance of Green Lantern; CGC FN/VF 7.0, sold for $1,434 in 2011.

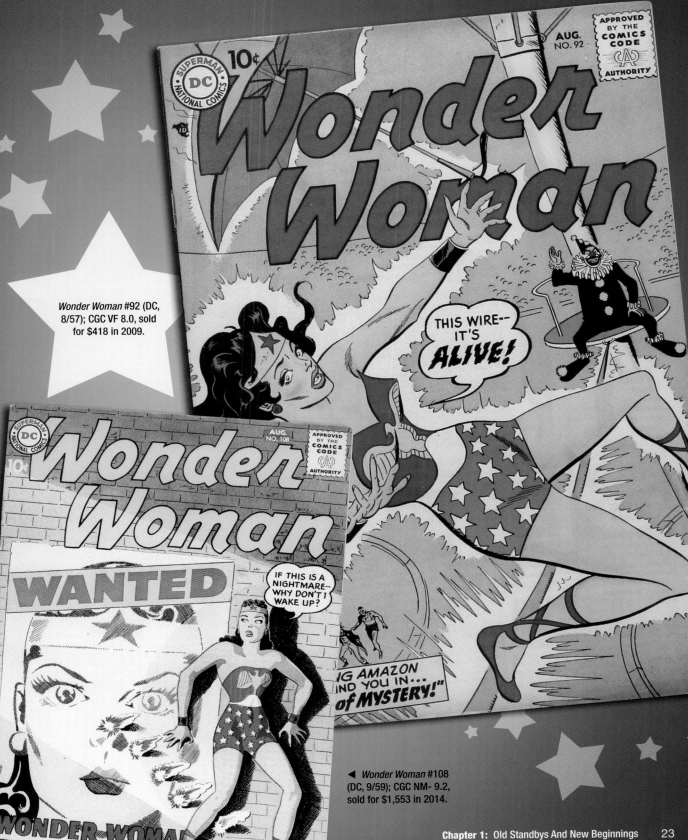

Wonder Woman #92 (DC, 8/57); CGC VF 8.0, sold for $418 in 2009.

◄ *Wonder Woman* #108 (DC, 9/59); CGC NM- 9.2, sold for $1,553 in 2014.

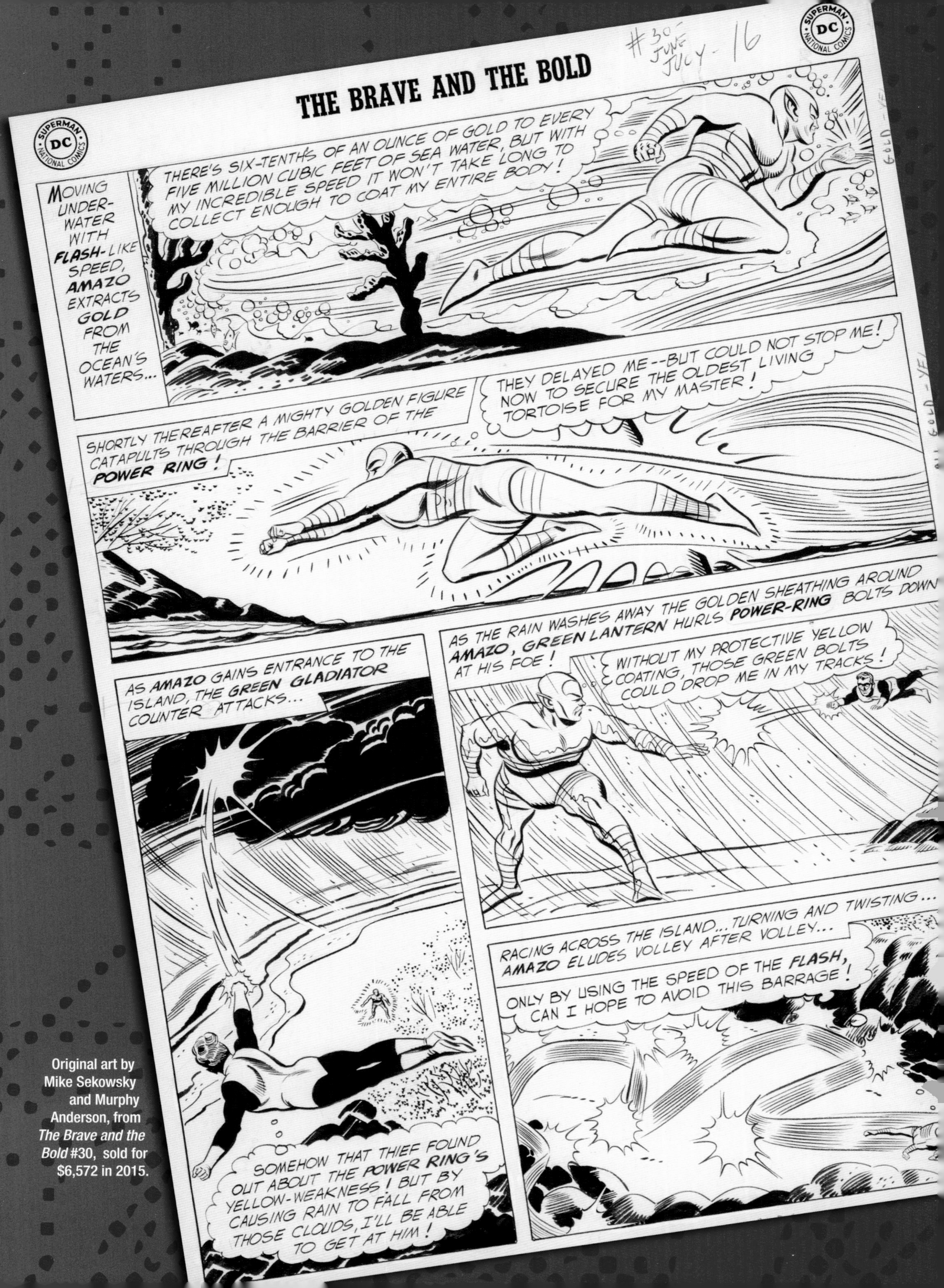

THE BRAVE AND THE BOLD
MOVING UNDER-WATER WITH FLASH-LIKE SPEED, AMAZO EXTRACTS GOLD FROM THE OCEAN'S WATERS...
THERE'S SIX-TENTHS OF AN OUNCE OF GOLD TO EVERY FIVE MILLION CUBIC FEET OF SEA WATER, BUT WITH MY INCREDIBLE SPEED IT WON'T TAKE LONG TO COLLECT ENOUGH TO COAT MY ENTIRE BODY!
SHORTLY THEREAFTER A MIGHTY GOLDEN FIGURE CATAPULTS THROUGH THE BARRIER OF THE POWER RING!
THEY DELAYED ME--BUT COULD NOT STOP ME! NOW TO SECURE THE OLDEST LIVING TORTOISE FOR MY MASTER!
AS AMAZO GAINS ENTRANCE TO THE ISLAND, THE GREEN GLADIATOR COUNTER ATTACKS...
SOMEHOW THAT THIEF FOUND OUT ABOUT THE POWER RING'S YELLOW-WEAKNESS! BUT BY CAUSING RAIN TO FALL FROM THOSE CLOUDS, I'LL BE ABLE TO GET AT HIM!
AS THE RAIN WASHES AWAY THE GOLDEN SHEATHING AROUND AMAZO, GREEN LANTERN HURLS POWER-RING BOLTS DOWN AT HIS FOE!
WITHOUT MY PROTECTIVE YELLOW COATING, THOSE GREEN BOLTS COULD DROP ME IN MY TRACKS!
RACING ACROSS THE ISLAND... TURNING AND TWISTING... AMAZO ELUDES VOLLEY AFTER VOLLEY...
ONLY BY USING THE SPEED OF THE FLASH, CAN I HOPE TO AVOID THIS BARRAGE!

Original art by Mike Sekowsky and Murphy Anderson, from *The Brave and the Bold* #30, sold for $6,572 in 2015.

CHAPTER 2

DC'S NEW FRONTIER: 1960-63

THE BEGINNING of the 1960s in America was an exciting time. The 1950s had been considered a conservative era, with Republican Dwight Eisenhower serving two terms as President. Old and stogy to many, Eisenhower did help launch the Space Age, but primarily as a way to compete with America's Cold War enemy, the Soviet Union. Many of Eisenhower's policies were in fact orchestrated by then-Vice President Richard Nixon, a right-wing conservative. Nixon was not well liked by many during this time, but with overwhelming support from the Republican Party, he announced his intention to run for President. Senator John F. Kennedy was youthful and charismatic, and his run for the Democratic nomination stirred up new hope for progressives. With Kennedy's election in November 1960, a "new frontier" was on the horizon. Things would move fast and change quickly during this halcyon time, and for those of us too young to really understand politics, comic books became the thing to read, and collect.

Following the success of DC's revival/retooling of The Flash and Green Lantern, editor Julie Schwartz reached back into his bag of Golden-Age goodies, and found two more heroes and a great team concept ready for a new look. First up would be the group.

One of the best-loved DC comics of the Golden Age was *All Star Comics*, featuring the Justice Society of America. This crime-fighting team consisted of the GA versions of The Flash, Green Lantern, Doctor Fate, Hour-Man, The Spectre, The Atom, Hawkman, Wonder Woman, The Sandman, Johnny Thunder, and Black Canary, in various combinations throughout the run of the series. The title ended in 1951 with issue #57, in the great purge of costumed comic book heroes.

Several major fans, chief among them the late Jerry Bails, wrote letters demanding the return of the JSA, and with the revised Flash and Green Lantern, Julie and original JSA writer Gardner Fox created the Justice League of America. The name change was explained by Julie, who said, "I'd like to do 'The Justice Society of America,' but I don't like the word 'Society,' because it's like a social group, and I want to use the word 'League,' because it's a more familiar word to young readers, like the National League (and) American League."

The new team would debut in another one of DC's anthology titles, *The Brave and the Bold*. Beginning in 1955, the comic featured a line-up of The Golden Gladiator, The Viking Prince, and The Silent Knight, none of whom were superhero in nature. This changed with issue #25 in 1959, which starred the original Suicide Squad (a team of adventurers, not the current super-villain concept). After two more Suicide Squad appearances, issue #28 introduced the new Justice League, with a roster including Martian Manhunter (an interplanetary crime fighter, introduced as a backup story in *Detective Comics* #225 in 1955); Wonder Woman, Aquaman, Superman, Green Lantern, Batman, and The Flash. This first appearance was an immediate hit, and the group would appear in two more consecutive issues of *Brave and the Bold* before their own title was launched, with a cover date of October 1960.

▲ DC's *The Brave and the Bold* issues #28, #29, and #30, first three appearances of the Justice League of America. These copies sold for, respectively: $31,070 (2010; CGC VF/NM 9.0), $38,240 (2015; CGC NM 9.4), and $4,541 (2015; CBCS VF/NM 9.0).

Since Hawkman had been such an integral part of the Justice Society (he was the only hero to appear in every story), he was a natural choice as the next GA hero to get a makeover. This occurred in *The Brave and the Bold* in a three-issue run beginning with #34. Around this same time, The Atom was the next DC hero of the 1940s to get a new look, new identity, and new powers with *Showcase* #34 (September-October 1961). Both would soon join the new Justice League.

The Brave and the Bold #34, first Silver Age Hawkman original cover artwork by Joe Kubert; sold for $89,625 in 2012.

▼ Showcase #34, (DC, 1961) first Silver Age appearance of The Atom, Curator pedigree copy; CGC NM- 9.2, sold for $1,314 in 2014.

◄ The Brave and the Bold #35 (DC, 1961), second Silver Age appearance of Hawkman; from the Don and Maggie Thompson Collection pedigree, CGC VF/NM 9.0, sold for $956 in 2016.

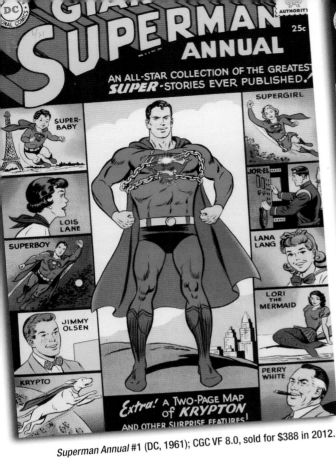

Superman Annual #1 (DC, 1961); CGC VF 8.0, sold for $388 in 2012.

Batman Annual #1 (DC, 1961); CGC VF/NM 9.0, sold for $956 in 2016.

A LOOK BACK, A LOOK AHEAD

One of the most important developments at DC was the repackaging of older stories, beginning with *Superman Annual* #1, which went on sale in early summer 1960. Until this time, publishers preferred to concentrate only on new material; it was assumed that comic readers during this time were children between eight and ten years old, and when they reached a certain age, they would move on to other interests. Thus, these older stories (most culled from the 1950s) were new to this young crop of readers.

The *Superman Annuals* were quickly followed by *Batman Annuals*, each 80 to 100 pages in size for a quarter. But perhaps the most important annual-sized comic from DC was called *Secret Origins*. Utilizing material from the new introductions of The Flash and Green Lantern, this hefty issue was filled with origin stories about the Superman-Batman team, Adam Strange (another interplanetary crime-busting sci-fi hero who was featured in *Strange Adventures*), Challengers of the

Secret Origins #1 (DC, 1961); CGC VF+ 8.5, sold for $763 in 2015.

The Flash #123 (DC, 9/61); first Silver Age appearance of the original Golden Age Flash, first Golden Age/Silver Age crossover event. CGC graded NM 9.4, this sold for $16,730 in 2009.

Unknown (an adventure team introduced just after The Flash in *Showcase*), Green Arrow, Wonder Woman, and Martian Manhunter (aka J'onn J'onzz). It was an instant primer for those new to the world of DC, and it was successful enough to warrant a sequel, *More Secret Origins*, in 1965.

Meanwhile, that crafty editor Julie Schwartz found a way to combine both versions of The Flash in *The Flash* #123 (September 1961). In this landmark story, Silver Age Flash Barry Allen accidentally transports himself to an alternate world, which just happens to be home to Jay Garrick, the original Golden Age Flash. Remember, our new version of the hero was seen reading an old issue of *Flash Comics* in his first story, so this "worlds colliding" tale came as a complete surprise to most fans. This issue, cover-titled "Flash of Two Worlds," is considered one of the most important comic books of the 1960s, and the concept of twin Earths ("Earth-One" where the modern-age heroes resided, and "Earth-Two," home of the now-aging heroes from the 1940s), was a wild success. This concept was carried over to Justice League, where it became an annual ritual to pair the old with the new, beginning with *Justice League of America* #21.

First two appearances of the Legion of Super-Heroes: *Adventure Comics* #247 (DC, 4/58), CGC VF/NM 9.0, sold for $11,352 in 2011; and *Adventure Comics* #267 (DC, 12/59); CGC VF 8.0, sold for $717 in 2010.

THE LEGION OF SUPER-HEROES

The Superman Family was growing stronger and stronger, thanks to offshoot titles. Superboy's flagship title, *Adventure Comics*, was now the home to the Legion of Super-Heroes. This series, set in the 30th Century (with a time-travelling Superboy as a charter member), saw its ranks expand with a slew of new, young protectors of the universe. Each member had at least one super power unique to the group: Triplicate Girl, who could split herself into three identical bodies (when one was killed in *Adventure Comics* #340, she became Duo Damsel); Phantom Girl (with the power of intangibility); Chameleon Boy (a shapeshifter, able to mimic any form); Colossal Boy (who could grow to any size); Invisible Kid (vanishing at will); Star Boy (he could increase the mass of any object); Brainiac 5 (super intelligence); Sun Boy (controls heat and light); Shrinking Violet (can reduce her size to microscopic); Bouncing Boy (could inflate himself and bounce around like a beach ball); Ultra Boy (all of Superboy's powers, but could use only one at a time); Mon-El (another Kryptonian with Superboy's powers; however, he spent several years trapped in the Phantom Zone); Matter-Eating Lad (can eat anything); Element Lad (transmutation); Lightning Lass (can control energy and electrical fields); and Dream Girl (and she was *quite* dreamy, with platinum-blonde hair; her power was precognition). Many more would follow, including a "Legion of Substitute Heroes" with oddball powers not deemed good enough to join the regular Legion (like Chlorophyll Kid, who had the ability to speed up the growth of any plant).

The Legion of Super-Heroes was a popular offshoot of the Superboy family of characters, and would stick around in one form or another for decades to come.

IN MY NEIGHBORHOOD

A comic I remember paying five cents for from the little grocery store down the street from my home in Houston.

FOR ME, 1961–63 WAS truly a Golden Age of comics. After I bought my first comic book off the stands (*Batman Annual* #1 – see introduction), I was immediately hooked, regularly spending my allowance on what started out as ten-cent items, but quickly rose to twelve cents.

They were still worth every penny I spent on them.

My comic-buying habits usually involved my family's weekly Friday night visit to the Lakewood Shopping Center, in the north part of Houston. The evening would often start at Dugan's Drug Store, located midway in the shopping complex, next door to Woolworth's. My mom and dad and I would have a hamburger dinner at the drug store's lunch counter (excellent old-style burgers and fries, washed down with cold cherry cokes). After that, Mom would go on to the grocery store, Dad would putter around, and I made a beeline to Dugan's newsstand area, where I would check out that week's comic book selections in a spinner rack, and for paperback book reprints of comic strips and the occasional *MAD Magazine*. My allowance back then was pretty small – only a quarter, unless I did a few extra chores, like weeding and edging around the house (a job I despised – spiders! – but did anyway, in order to have a little more spending money). I usually brought home only a couple of comics, and I wasted no time reading them when I got to my bedroom.

From time to time, I would also buy comics at a nearby convenience store, one that seemed to have a few comic books I couldn't find at Dugan's, and I would walk down to Mrs. Harmon's little grocery store several times a week to check out her stack of used comics, priced at a nickel each.

I didn't have many friends at the time who shared my passion, but across from our house was the home of the Grayson's. Becky Grayson was my age, and her sister, Bonnie, was a year or so older, and they were both voracious readers. I can thank Becky and Bonnie for turning me on to Lois Lane, a title I probably would not have gotten into on my own (as well as other "girl" comics like *Little Lulu*, and Disney titles like *Uncle Scrooge*).

It didn't take long for me to get a pretty sizable collection together, a stack of comics I kept in my closet. I was pretty finicky about how I handled my books – no folding the pages back like some young readers. In time, visiting Houston-area cousins and a few friends discovered my stashed-away stack. I soon came to hate it when they would come over, because all they wanted to do was grab a few comics and sit down to read, rather than go outside and play in our oversized back yard. The only point in my favor was I got to do the same whenever I went to their house to visit or spend the night!

POP CULTURE EVENTS, 1960-64

MAY 1960 . . . . . . Russia shoots down American U-2 Spy Plane flown by Francis Gary Powers

AUGUST 1960 . . . Novelty song, "Itsy Bitsy Teenie Weenie Yellow Polkadot Bikini," hits #1 on the pop charts

OCTOBER 1960 . . . *The Andy Griffith Show* and *Route 66* premiere on CBS-TV

NOVEMBER 1960 . John F. Kennedy elected President

MAY 1961 . . . . Alan Shepard becomes the first American in space

MARCH 1961 . . . . . The Beatles perform at the Cavern Club (Liverpool) for the first time

AUGUST 1961 . . . . Berlin Wall construction begins

DECEMBER 1961 . . The Vietnam War officially begins

FEBRUARY 1962 . . John Glenn becomes first American to orbit the Earth

MARCH 1962 . . . . Bob Dylan releases his first album

JULY 1962 . . . . . . First Walmart store opens; The Rolling Stones debut at London's Marquee Club

AUGUST 1962 . . . . Marilyn Monroe dies; Ringo Starr joins The Beatles

SEPTEMBER 1962 . Animated series *The Jetsons* premieres on ABC

OCTOBER 1962 . . . Johnny Carson begins hosting *The Tonight Show*; *Dr. No*, the first James Bond movie, opens in the UK; Cuban Missile Crisis occurs

DECEMBER 1962 . . Mariner 2 transmits data from Venus

JANUARY 1963 . . Animated TV series *Astro Boy* debuts in Japan

MARCH 1963 . . . . The Beatles release their first album, *Please Please Me*, in the UK; Alfred Hitchcock's classic movie *The Birds* opens

JULY 1963 . . . . . . The Zip Code is introduced by the United States Postal Service

AUGUST 1963 . . . The Great Train Robbery occurs in the UK; Martin Luther King delivers his "I have a dream" speech in Washington, D.C.

NOVEMBER 1963 . President John F. Kennedy is assassinated; Lyndon B. Johnson becomes President; *Doctor Who* premieres on British TV

DECEMBER 1963 . The Beatles release "I Want to Hold Your Hand" in the US

JANUARY 1964 . . Roald Dahl publishes *Charlie and the Chocolate Factory*

FEBRUARY 1964 . The Beatles arrive in the US and appear on *The Ed Sullivan Show*

MARCH 1964 . . . . Boxer Cassius Clay changes his name to Muhammad Ali; the Ford Mustang is introduced; the Great Alaskan Earthquake occurs

APRIL 1964 . . . . . Sidney Portier becomes the first African-American to win Best Actor Oscar; Shea Stadium opens in New York; New York World's Fair opens

JULY 1964 . . . . . . Civil Rights Bill enacted, abolishing segregation in the US

AUGUST 1964 . . . The final Looney Tunes cartoon, *Senorella and the Glass Huarache*, is released the theaters; Disney's *Mary Poppins* opens

SEPTEMBER 1964 . TV series *Bewitched*, *Shindig*, and animated *Jonny Quest* debut

DECEMBER 1964 . The Berkeley Free Speech Movement sit-in protest occurs, with 800 students arrested; stop-motion TV special *Rudolph the Red-Nosed Reindeer* debuts

'Swinging Lunch Time Rock Sessions'
AT THE
LIVERPOOL JAZZ SOCIETY,
13, TEMPLE STREET (off Dale Street and Victoria Street).
EVERY LUNCH TIME, 12-00 to 2-30
RESIDENT BANDS:
Gerry and the Pacemakers,
Rory Storm and the Wild Ones,
The Big Three.

Next Wednesday Afternoon, March 15th
12-00 to 5-00 Special
STARRING—
The Beatles,
Gerry and the Pacemakers
Rory Storm and the Wild Ones.
Admission—Members 1/-, Visitors 1/6
"Rocking at the L. J. S."
The Vector Printing Co. 238, West Derby Road, Liverpool, 6

SUPERMAN COMIC BOOKS, 1960-61

Superman #139 (DC, 8/60); CGC VF/NM 9.0, sold for $776 in 2016.

▲ *Superman* #138 (DC, 7/60); CGC VF/NM 9.0, sold for $1,673 in 2015.

▶ *Superman Annual* #2 (DC, 1961); CGC NM- 9.2, sold for $836 in 2009.

▼ *Superman's Pal Jimmy Olsen* #44 (DC, 4/60); CGC VF+ 8.5, sold for $437 in 2012.

▲ *Superman's Pal Jimmy Olsen* #53 (DC, 6/61); CGC NM- 9.2, sold for $1,195 in 2014.

◀ *Superman's Girl Friend Lois Lane* #21 (DC, 11/60); CGC NM+ 9.6, sold for $1,792 in 2010.

SUPERMAN IN ACTION COMICS, 1960-64

▼ Action Comics #300 (DC, 5/63); CGC NM+ 9.6, sold for $1,434 in 2012.

Action Comics #294 (DC, 11/62); CGC NM 9.4, sold for $1,553 in 2011.

Action Comics #269 (DC, 10/60); CGC NM- 9.2, sold for $382 in 2016.

Original cover art to *Action Comics* #315 (DC, 8/64) by Curt Swan and George Kline; sold for $32,265 in 2013.

Adventure Comics #280 (DC, 1/61); CGC NM+ 9.6, so $1,254 in 2010.

▶ *Superboy* #79 (DC, 3/60); CGC FN+ 6.5, sold for $47 in 2010.

SUPERBOY AND ADVENTURE COMICS, 1960-64

Adventure Comics #327 (DC, 12/64); Twin Cities pedigree copy, CGC NM+ 9.6, sold for $418 in 2012.

Superboy #86 (DC, 1/61); CGC NM 9.4, sold for $2,390 in 2010.

Adventure Comics #312 (DC, 9/63); CGC NM 9.4, sold for $1,474 in 2010.

Adventure Comics #319 (DC, 4/64); CGC NM+ 9.6, sold for $1,234 in 2010.

SUPERGIRL, 1960-64

▲ *Superman's Girl Friend Lois Lane* #20 (DC, 10/60); CGC NM- 9.2, sold for $507 in 2010.

◄ *Action Comics* #285 (DC, 2/62); CGC NM 9.4, sold for $1,195 in 2011.

Action Comics #262 (DC, 3/60); CGC NM 9.4, sold for $956 in 2013.

World's Finest Comics #108 (DC, 3/60); CGC NM 9.4, sold for $1,314 in 2012.

The Brave and the Bold #54 (DC, 7/64); first Teen Titans appearance; Don and Maggie Thompson pedigree copy, CGC NM+ 9.6, sold for $7,179 in 2014.

◄ *The Brave and the Bold* #51 (DC, 12/63); Twin Cities pedigree copy, CGC NM- 9.2, sold for $442 in 2013.

Original splash page art by Howard Purcell for *Brave and the Bold* #51; sold for $1,750 in 2008.

Adventure Comics #275 (DC, 8/60); CGC NM 9.4, sold for $956 in 2010.

Batman #134 (DC, 9/60); CGC NM- 9.2, sold for $567 in 2010.

Batman #156 (DC, 6/63); CGC NM- 9.2, sold for $836 in 2014.

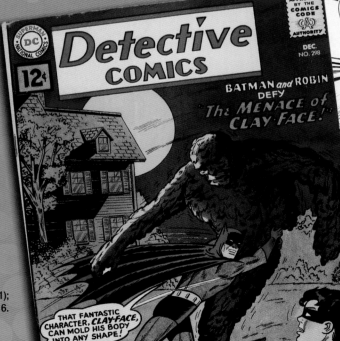

▶ Detective Comics #298 (DC, 12/61);
CGC VF+ 8.5, sold for $525 in 2016.

Original splash page art by Sheldon Moldoff and Charles Paris for *Batman* #144; sold for $3,346 in 2008.

Detective Comics #322 (DC, 12/63); CGC NM+ 9.6, sold for $1,553 in 2011.

'NEW LOOK' BATMAN, 1964

▶ *Detective Comics* #330 (DC, 8/64); Twin Cities pedigree copy, CGC NM- 9.2, sold for $215 in 2012.

Batman #168 (DC, 12/64); CGC NM 9.4, sold for $418 in 2010.

Detective Comics #331 (DC, 9/64); CGC NM- 9.2, sold for $215 in 2015.

▲ *Batman* #164 (DC, 6/64);
CGC VF/NM 9.0, sold for $167 in 2015.

▼ Original splash page art by Sheldon Moldoff and Joe Giella
for *Detective Comics* #352; sold for $5,975 in 2012.

JUSTICE LEAGUE OF AMERICA, 1960-64

Justice League of America #1 (DC, 10-11/60); CGC VF- 7.5, sold for $4,541 in 2015.

I'VE GOT THIS GAME RIGGED SO THAT EVERY-TIME *FLASH* MAKES A MOVE, A MEMBER OF THE *JUSTICE LEAGUE* DISAPPEARS FROM THE FACE OF THE EARTH!

A COMPLETE BOOK-LENGTH NOVEL *FEATURING* THE WORLD'S GREATEST HEROES! *"SLAVE SHIP of SPACE!"*

BACK AFTER 12 YEARS! THE LEGENDARY SUPER-STARS OF THE JUSTICE SOCIETY OF *America!*

Featuring "CRISIS ON EARTH-ONE!"

Justice League of America #21 (DC, 8/63); CBCS VF/NM 9.0, sold for $717 in 2016.

◄ Justice League of America #3 (DC, 2-3/61); CGC NM 9.4, sold for $8,962 in 2010.

▲ Cover art by Carmine Infantino and Joe Giella for *The Flash* #117 (DC, 12/60); sold for $71,700 in 2013.

▲ *The Flash* #139 (DC, 9/63); CGC NM 9.4, sold for $5,736 in 2015.

▶ *The Flash* #128 (DC, 5/62); Western Penn pedigree copy, CGC VF/ NM 9.0, sold for $956 in 2009.

Original page 16 from *Green Lantern* #12, by Gil Kane and Joe Giella; sold for $3,226 in 2014.

Green Lantern #1 (DC, 8/60); CGC NM 9.4, sold for $50,787 in 2010.

Green Lantern #8 (DC, 10/61); Don and Maggie Thompson pedigree copy, CGC NM 9.4, sold for $2,629 in 2014.

Green Lantern #32 (DC, 10/64); Pacific Coast pedigree copy, CGC NM+ 9.6, sold for $1,792 in 2013.

◀ *Aquaman* #18 (DC, 11-12/64); Don/Maggie Thompson pedigree copy, CGC NM 9.4, sold for $274 in 2014.

The Atom #1 (DC, 6-7/62); CGC NM- 9.2, sold for $2,868 in 2015.

◀ *Aquaman* #1 (DC, 1-2/62); CGC NM- 9.2, sold for $6,572 in 2015.

Original page 14 from *Showcase* #35 featuring The Atom, by Gil Kane and Murphy Anderson; sold for $1,434 in 2012.

▼ *The Atom* #10 (DC, 12/63-1/64); Twin Cities pedigree copy, CGC NM 9.4, sold for $388 in 2011.

Hawkman #1 (DC, 4-5/64); Twin Cities pedigree copy, CGC NM+ 9.6, sold for $4,481 in 2014.

Hawkman #2 (DC, 6-7/64); CGC NM 9.4, sold for $549 in 2016.

WONDER WOMAN, 1961–64

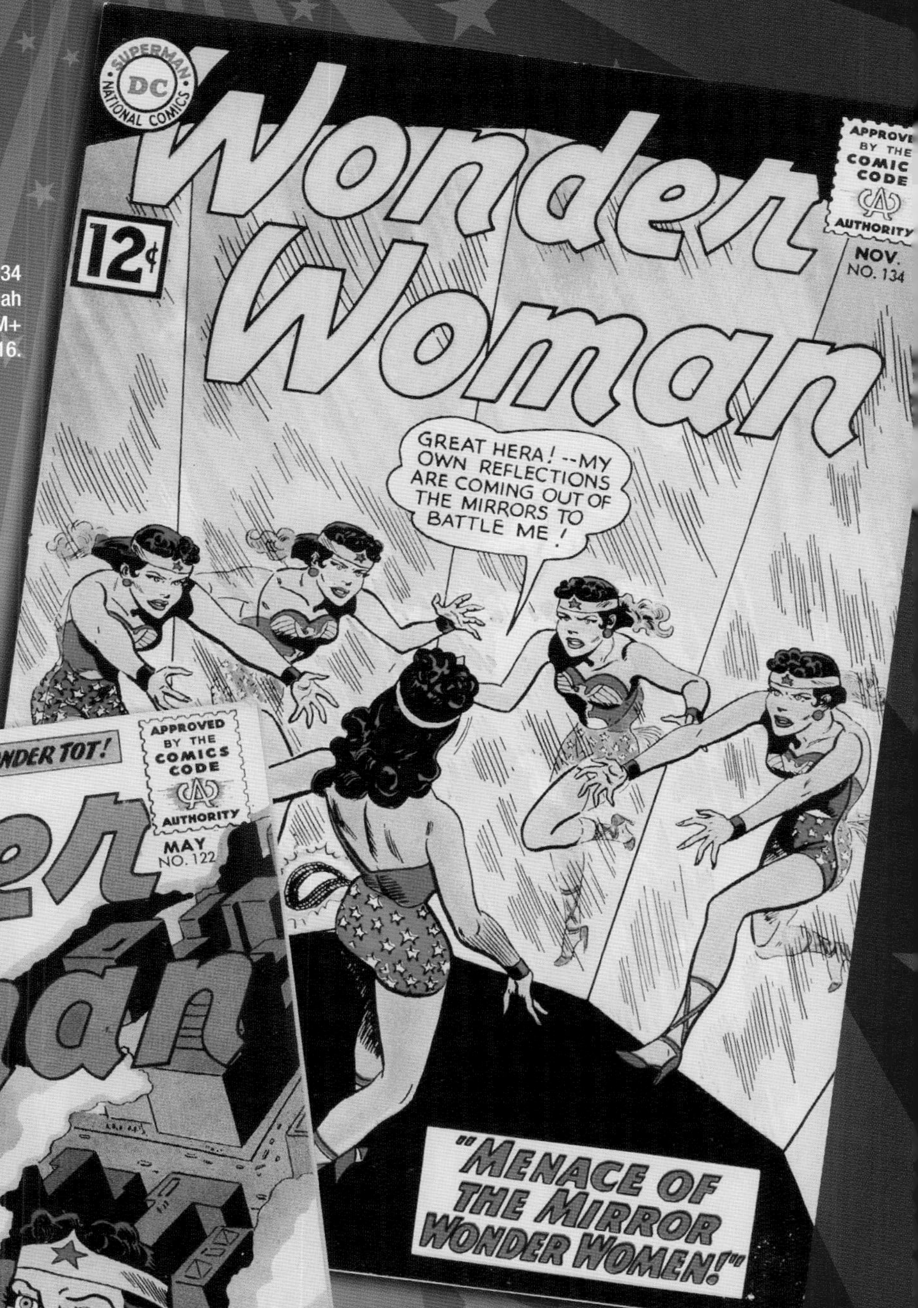
SUPERMAN
DC
NATIONAL COMICS
Wonder Woman
APPROVED BY THE COMIC CODE AUTHORITY
12¢
NOV. NO. 134
GREAT HERA! --MY OWN REFLECTIONS ARE COMING OUT OF THE MIRRORS TO BATTLE ME!
"MENACE OF THE MIRROR WONDER WOMEN!"

Wonder Woman #134 (DC, 11/1962); Savannah pedigree copy, CGC NM+ 9.6, sold for $525 in 2016.

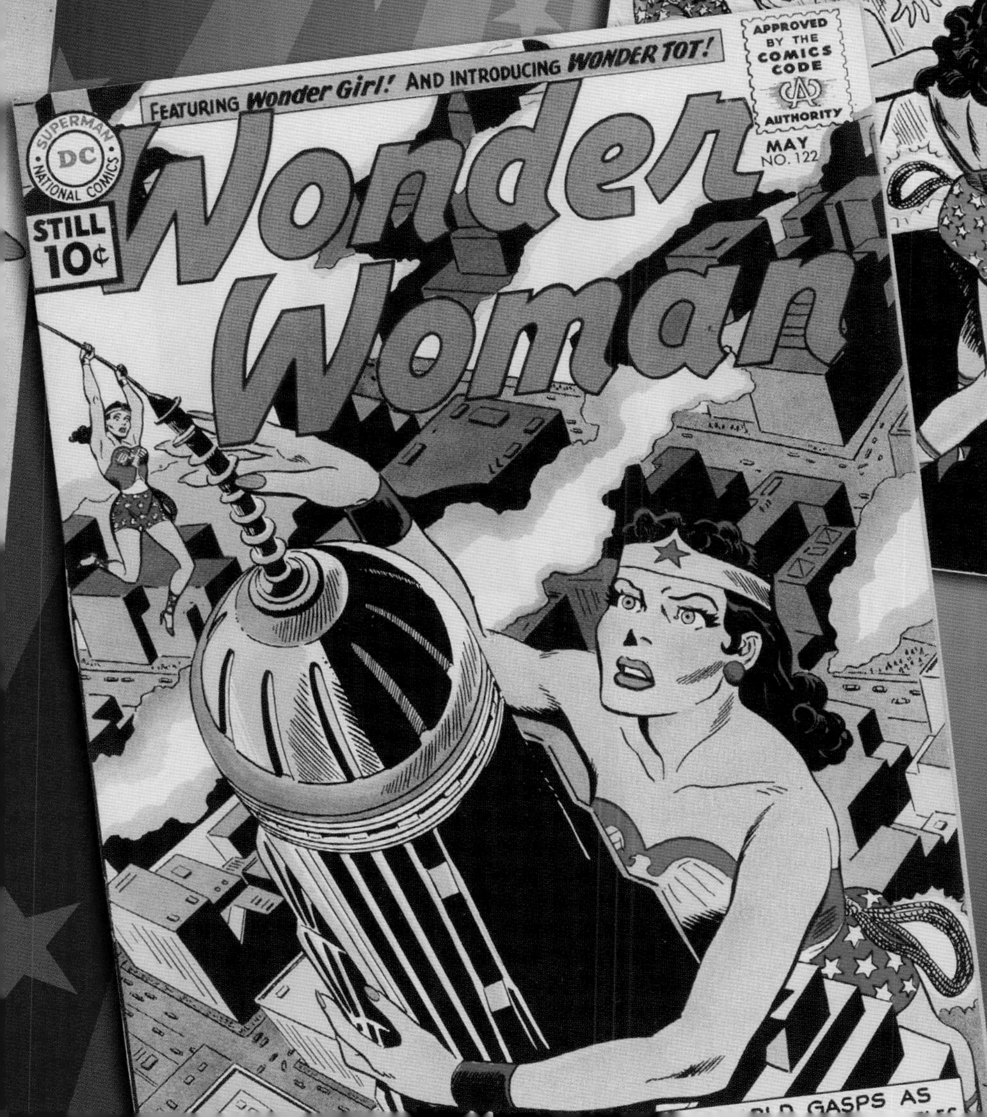
FEATURING Wonder Girl! AND INTRODUCING WONDER TOT!
APPROVED BY THE COMICS CODE AUTHORITY
MAY NO. 122
SUPERMAN
DC
NATIONAL COMICS
STILL 10¢
Wonder Woman

Wonder Woman #122 (DC, 5/61); Savannah pedigree copy, CGC NM 9.4, sold for $573 in 2016.

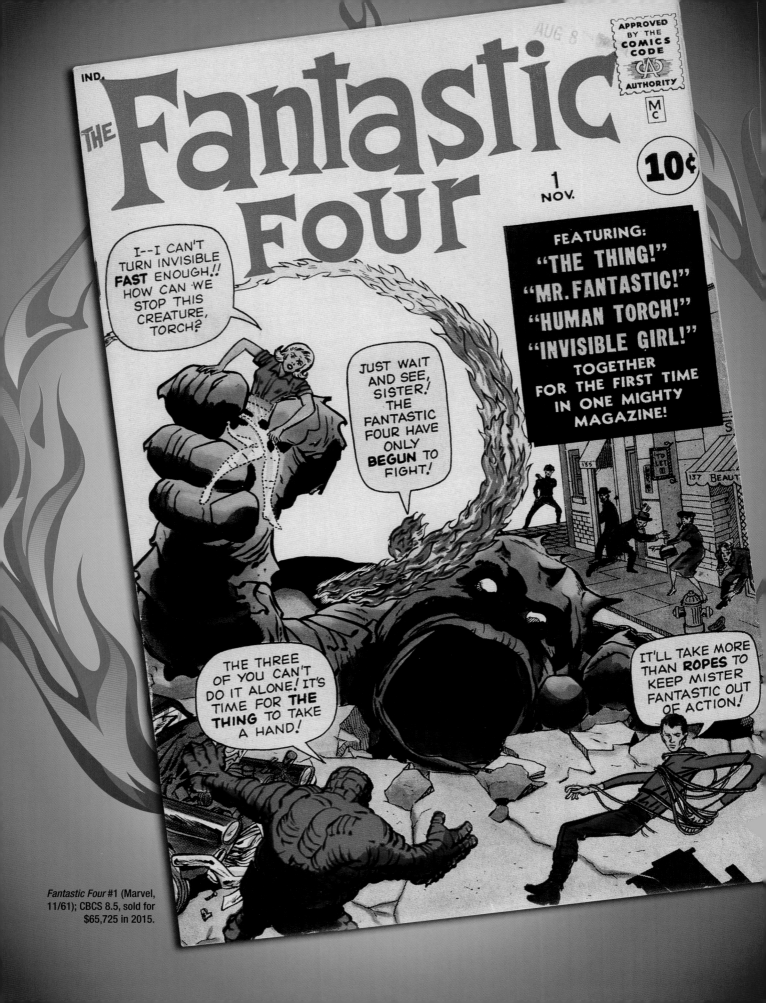

Fantastic Four #1 (Marvel, 11/61); CBCS 8.5, sold for $65,725 in 2015.

CHAPTER 3

THE NEW HOUSE OF iDEAS: MARVEL, 1961-64

MARTiN GOODMAN'S publishing company was in the comic book business from almost the very start. His New York City-based operation began with pulp magazines in 1933, before launching the Timely line of comics in 1939 with the publication of *Marvel Comics* #1. Like most Golden Age comic book companies, the original focus was on costumed superheroes, until the post-war hero slump whittled away the mystery men in favor of teen humor, crime, funny animal, war, and other then-trendy topics. Within a relatively short span of years, the Timely heroes — Captain America, the Human Torch, and Sub-Mariner were the big three — would fade away, their titles taken over by horror stories inspired by the success of EC. Timely heroic comics were among the most patriotic during World War II, with many issues sporting a cover by Alex Schomburg, Al Avision, or Syd Shores featuring Japanese or Nazi Germany villains being thwarted by the Human Torch melting through their bunkers to save trussed-up women or kids from unspeakable torture, or a larger-than-life Sub-Mariner crushing enemy war ships. Captain America simply used his fists to pummel away at the bad guys.

Goodman had tried to revive Timely's biggest heroes for his mid-fifties line (now being called Atlas) to fight Cold-War communists, but the effort lasted only a few issues. Soon, outrageous monsters and other sci-fi-inspired stories filled the pages of *Tales of Suspense* and *Journey Into Mystery*. This would continue throughout the late 1950s.

However, Goodman had been watching as DC successfully revived The Flash and Green Lantern. In particular, it was the runaway success of DC's team-oriented Justice League of America that got the wheels of change turning for what would, in time, become the most popular superhero comics of the 1960s.

Peter Parker, as drawn by Steve Ditko.

Goodman's wife, Jean, had a young cousin who needed a job in the early 1940s, Stan Lee (born Stanley Martin Lieber, in 1922). Lee was hired and stayed with the company, working his way up the corporate ladder. Lee was doing a lot of writing for the Timely and Atlas titles, and with Goodman's blessing, wrote a story involving a group of adventurers who, after an accidental exposure to cosmic rays during a space flight, developed strange new powers. The script was handed to artist Jack Kirby (who had been instrumental in creating Timely's biggest hero, Captain America), and The Fantastic Four was born.

Stan Lee's genius was in creating hip-sounding dialogue, and in making his characters realistic in a way his young readers could identify with — slightly flawed real people who happened, by accident, to have acquired super powers; still, they were people with real-life problems, fears, hopes, and desires. Stan's brilliant idea was to present his characters as ordinary, often-flawed individuals who find themselves in extraordinary situations. The Fantastic Four was more a family than just another group of crime-fighters in tight suits. The group consisted of Reed Richards, the oldest member and a scientific genius (as Mr. Fantastic, with a Plastic Man-like ability to stretch himself into just about any length or shape); his young girlfriend Sue Storm (aka The Invisible Woman); Sue's hot-headed teenage brother, Johnny (inheriting the powers of Golden Age Timely hero, The Human Torch); and curmudgeonly ex-college football star, Ben Grimm (the grotesque but enormously powerful creature called The Thing). This new group of heroes squabbled with each other and held petty grudges (like real people do) before coming together to defeat some fantastic enemy. Their down-to-earth demeanor was refreshingly different from the somewhat aloof attitude DC's heroes seemed to sometimes have, lending a real air of credibility to kids who argued with their siblings, parents, friends, and, from time to time, their teachers. They were fantastically powered, but in many ways, "just like us," with every day, relatable problems.

The debut of *Fantastic Four* #1 (cover-dated November, 1961) was a big success for the company, now known as Marvel Comics. The

The first appearance of Spider-Man, with cover art by Jack Kirby. This near-perfect copy, CGC graded NM 9.4, was sold by Heritage Auctions for the astronomical sum of $454,100 in 2016.

best was yet to come, though, and it soon arrived as the cover feature for *Amazing Fantasy* #15 (August-September, 1962). Issues #1-14 had been titled *Amazing Adult Fantasy*, with sci-fi story content, but issue #15 was meant as a new direction, with superhero stories added to the mix. A new hero was developed for *Amazing Fantasy*, another creation of Stan Lee's called Spider-Man (that's right — "Spider-Man" with a hyphen, not "Spiderman" as most fans would refer to him at the time). Jack Kirby would help develop the origin of Spider-Man as a typical mixed-up teenage student who is accidentally bitten by a spider exposed to radiation at a science exhibit. Kirby drew a few pages, but apparently they looked "too heroic" to Stan. Artist Steve Ditko, who had been handling sci-fi and monster stories with his unique fine-line style, was brought in, and the rest is honest-to-goodness comic book history.

Spider-Man had a great backstory that set the tone for the series. Peter Parker was a "science nerd" high school student who lived with his kindly Aunt May and Uncle Ben in New York. After discovering his new powers, the

gadget-minded Peter concocts an adhesive substance he can shoot out like webbing through wrist-worn devices. After making himself a stylized red and dark blue costume, he sets out on capitalizing his newfound abilities by appearing as a daredevil stunt man. On his way home from such a gig, he ignores cries to stop a thief. "Sorry pal! That's *your* job!" he says to a policeman on the scene. "I'm through being pushed around — by anyone! From now on I just look out for number one — that means, *me*!" This indifference catches up to him when Peter discovers the very same criminal he failed to stop has mugged — and killed — his beloved Uncle Ben. Peter now realizes that "with great power, there must also come great responsibility" and sets out on a career as a superhero crime-fighter. Of course, the public misunderstands him and considers this masked man a threat, largely thanks to the editorial musings of J. Jonah Jameson, newspaper publisher. This is all compounded by the fact that Peter has been hired by the newspaper for his incredible photos of Spider-Man in action (taken with an automatic camera suspended in place by webbing).

◀ Spider-Man in action! From *Amazing Spider-Man* #10, page 17; art by Steve Ditko.

Incredible Hulk #1 (Marvel, 5/62); CGC VF+ 8.5, sold for $58,256 in 2010.

Journey Into Mystery #83, the first Thor (Marvel, 8/62); CBCS NM+ 9.6, sold for $215,100 in 2015.

Spider-Man was a real mind-blower to most comic-reading kids in 1962, and was an immediate hit. The new Marvel Age of comics had begun in earnest, with a great stable of colorful superheroes, including:

- Prince Namor, the Sub-Mariner — revised version of the Golden Age Timely character; he first appeared in *Fantastic Four* #4 (May, 1962)
- The Incredible Hulk — first appeared in *The Incredible Hulk* #1 (May, 1962)
- The Mighty Thor — first appeared in *Journey into Mystery* #83 (August, 1962)
- Iron Man — first appeared in *Tales of Suspense* #39 (March, 1963)
- The X-Men — first appeared in *The X-Men* #1 (September, 1963)

- Dr. Strange — first appeared in *Strange Tales* #110 (July, 1963)
- Daredevil — first appeared in *Daredevil* #1 (April, 1964)

On this page and the next are the first appearances and first issues of five of the most popular Marvel superheroes. The price they sold for at auction is also not too shabby for comic books originally priced at twelve cents each!

THE AVENGERS

Marvel's next team of powerful heroes was The Avengers, which debuted with *The Avengers* #1 in September 1963 with a line-up that first included Thor, Iron Man, The Wasp, The Hulk, and Ant-Man (originally introduced in *Tales to Astonish* #27, cover-dated January 1962, in

Tales of Suspense #39, first Iron Man (Marvel, 3/63); CGC NM+ 9.6, sold for $262,900 in 2015.

X-Men #1 (Marvel, 9/63); CGC NM 9.4, sold for $83,650 in 2013.

Daredevil #1 (Marvel, 4/64); CGC NM+ 9.6, sold for $37,343 in 2012.

BIG-SCREEN SUPERHEROES

THESE CHARACTERS HAVE BOX-OFFICE POWER

Some of the biggest superheroes of the Silver Age are now stars of the Silver Screen's most successful movie franchises that have grossed billions of dollars. Batman boasts the biggest and baddest superhero franchise of all time (see Chapter 4), but these other heroes are no slouches, either, when it comes to taking your money.

Although not technically a franchise yet, based on the whopping success of her self-titled debut movie in 2017 and a sequel apparently planned for 2019, Wonder Woman may end up with one — last year's *Wonder Woman* raked in $412.5 million domestically. And with *Justice League* hauling in $212 million domestically as of December 2017, after its release date of Nov. 17, it may earn a sequel and maybe a future franchise as well.

Superheroes will remain big in 2018, with these movies hitting the screen: *Black Panther* (February), *The New Mutants* (April), *Avengers: Infinity War* (May), *Deadpool 2* (June), *Ant-Man and The Wasp* (July), *Venom* (October), *X-Men: Dark Phoenix* (November) *Aquaman* (December).

As of December 2017, here is how the movie franchises of The Avengers, Captain America, The Fantastic Four, Iron Man, The X-Men, Spider-Man, Superman, and Thor stack up at the Box Office. **Note**: These numbers are based off of domestic gross income reported at Box Office Mojo (boxofficemojo.com).

1. X-MEN: $2.4 BILLION

Professor X and his band of mutants including Wolverine, Jean Grey, Rogue, and Cyclops, have been a huge name in comics for more than 50 years and have also been conquering cinema complexes since the first movie, *X-Men*, hit the big screen in 2000. Three new additions to the franchise expected to be released in 2018, *X-Men: Dark Phoenix*, *X-Men: New Mutants*, and *Deadpool* 2, will give another huge boost to the franchise that already includes these nine movies and their earnings: *X-Men* (2000; $257,983,200), *X2: X-Men United* (2003; $315,117,000), *X-Men: The Last Stand* (2006; $316,299,900), *X-Men Origins: Wolverine* (2009; $213,159,100), *X-Men: First Class* (2011; $160,754,100), *The Wolverine* (2013; $149,359,800), *X-Men: Days of Future Past* (2014; $248,695,700), *X-Men: Apocalypse* (2016; $157,475,600), *Deadpool* (2016; $373, 869, 900), *Logan* (2017; $226,275,000).

2. SPIDER-MAN: $2.4 BILLION

Of the six movies in this franchise, the first one, 2002's *Spider-Man*, remains the cornerstone, earning $614,245,200. Here is how the other films fared: *Spider-Man 2* (2004; $531,803,300), *Spider-Man 3* (2007; $432,402,300), *The Amazing Spider-Man* (2012; $297,713,000), *The Amazing Spider-Man 2* (2014; $215,371, 800), and *Spider-Man: Homecoming* (2017; $334,201,1440).

3. SUPERMAN: $1.9 BILLION

Although it was released 40 years ago, the original *Superman* (1978) is still the top Box Office earner with $507,045,800. The other movies: *Superman 2* (1981; $344,015,000), *Superman 3* (1983; $168,242,400), *Superman 4: The Quest for Peace* (1987; $35,452,700), *Superman Returns* (2006; $270,033,2004), *Man of Steel* (2013; $307,021,800), and *Batman v Superman: Dawn of Justice* (2016; $338,224,000).

4. IRON MAN: $1.1 BILLION

Tony Stark is the most popular Avenger for many people and in the movie realm, he keeps drawing more in. The third movie and second sequel in the franchise, *Iron Man 3* (2013), is the top earner with $431,465,800. The others: *Iron Man* (2008; $392,017,400) and *Iron Man 2* (2010; $347,410,100).

5. THE AVENGERS: $1.1 BILLION

One of the most successful ensemble superhero franchises of all time, The Avengers will become even bigger with the release of *Avengers: Infinity War* in April 2018 and another movie in the works for 2019. The first two movies in the franchise stack up as thus: *Marvel's The Avengers* (2012; $679,629,900) and *Avengers: Age of Ultron* (2015; $473,177,900).

6. CAPTAIN AMERICA: $885.7 MILLION

Another popular Avenger, Captain America has generated nearly $1 billion in box office earnings with the trio of movies in the franchise, with each one raking in more than the last: *Captain America: The First Avenger* (2011; $196,705,900), *Captain America: The Winter Soldier* (2014; $275,767,300), and *Captain America: Civil War* (2016; $413,316,300).

7. THOR: $723.6 MILLION

The Norse god of thunder and lightning and his trusty Mjolnir conquer the box office every time a new movie comes out. The third movie in the franchise, *Thor: Ragnarok*, released in November 2017, is the top earner, with $306,375,120 as of mid-December 2017. This is how the first two films stack up: *Thor* (2011; $198,608,000) and *Thor: The Dark World* (2013; $218,709,200).

8. THE FANTASTIC FOUR: $442.9 MILLION

A trio of movies starring the fantastic Reed Richards, Sue Richards, Benjamin Grimm, and Johnny Storm has helped make this one of the top franchises. The first movie, 2005's *Fantastic Four*, is the top grosser with $213,340,600. Here's how the other two stack up: *Fantastic Four: Rise of the Silver Surfer* (2007; $169,504,100), and the reboot *Fantastic Four* (2015;112,000).

a story titled "The Man in the Ant Hill"). With issue #4 (March 1964), the two worlds of Golden Age Timely and Silver Age Marvel came together with the reintroduction of the original Captain America, who was found floating in the sea, suspended within an iceberg. Cap had made one earlier try-out appearance in *Strange Tales* #114 (November 1963), but that turned out to be an imposter. With the Original Cap back in action, now as part of the Avengers, the Marvel line was rock-solid and ready to kick some comic book ass. Look out, DC!

JACK KIRBY AND STEVE DITKO

The early sixties success of Marvel wasn't just from Stan Lee's scripts. There were many talented artists who worked for Marvel during this time, but there were two powerhouse artists who helped turn this one-time "second rate" comics publisher into one of the top two (and

Page of original artwork by Jack Kirby and Paul Reinman, from *The Avengers* #2 (Marvel, 1963); sold for $5,676 in 2011.

I have to admit that in the beginning of my love affair with comic books, I wasn't much of a Marvel fan. I do remember buying a copy of *Amazing Spider-Man* #1 off a spinner rack, but at the time, Steve Ditko's artwork didn't do much for this young fan accustomed to the clean line work of Curt Swan. I realize this will sound like blasphemy to some fans, but I cared even less for Jack Kirby's art, at least back then. At the time, the Marvel line was aimed at slightly older readers than me, and I'll admit it – it was all over my head in the early sixties. Since then, I have, of course, come to love this material, but in 1961-64, I was buying just about everything off the stands *except* Marvel. Live and learn, right True Believers?

there are many who would say Marvel was *numero uno* during the sixties).

First, Jack Kirby. Jack had been in the business since the mid-1930s, and was instrumental in creating one of the greatest of all comic book heroes — Captain America, in 1941 (with his partner, Joe Simon). Jack had worked pretty much non-stop from the start, jumping from

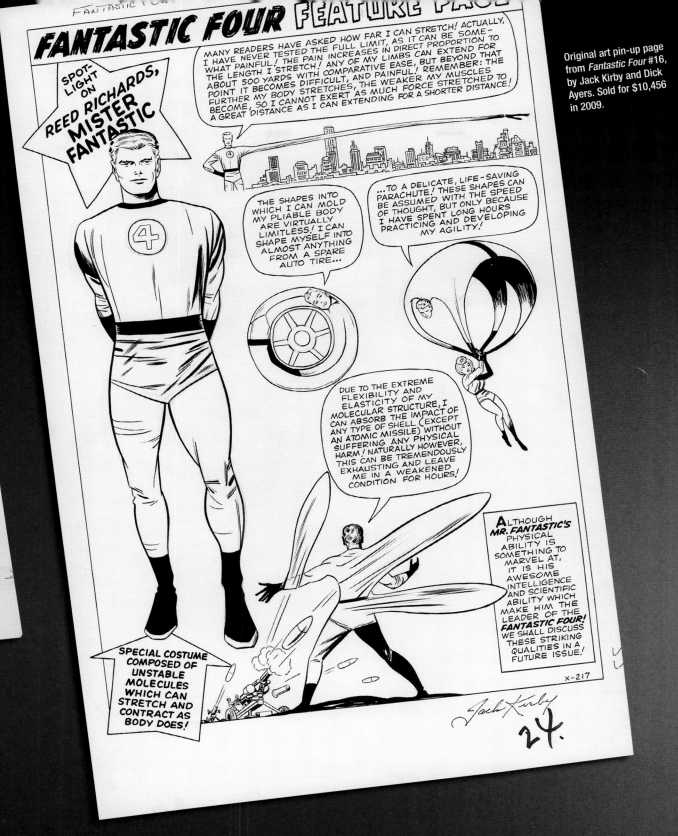

one publisher to another. He spent part of the early Silver Age at DC, where he handled art chores on *Challengers of the Unknown* and various mystery/suspense stories for titles like *House of Mystery*, plus a handful of Green Arrow backup

stories that appeared in *Adventure Comics* and *World's Finest Comics*. In the late '50s, he was at Atlas, cranking out monster stories for *Amazing Adventures*, *Strange Tales*, *World of Fantasy* and other similar titles. When Stan Lee developed his Fantastic Four concept, it was Kirby who got the art assignment. Kirby had a way with depicting action scenes like no one else in the business, and he went all out with the FF. He also assisted other artists at Marvel by doing page "breakdowns" (layouts). Artist Gil Kane summed it up nicely: "Jack was the single most influential figure in the turnaround in Marvel's fortunes from the time he rejoined the company ... It wasn't merely that Jack conceived most of the characters that are being done, but ... Jack's point of view and philosophy of drawing became the governing philosophy of the entire publishing company and, beyond the publishing company, of the entire field ... [Marvel took] Jack and use[d] him as a primer. They would get artists ... and they taught them the ABCs, which amounted to learning Jack Kirby. Jack was like the Holy Scripture and they simply had to follow him without deviation. That's what was told to me ... It was how they taught everyone to reconcile all those opposing attitudes to one single master point of view." *(Source: Gil Kane, speaking at a forum on July 6, 1985, at the Dallas Fantasy Fair.)*

The second artist is Steve Ditko. Steve had been working steadily throughout the fifties for several companies, including "poverty row" publisher Charlton. He specialized in science fiction, but was at home with just about any genre. He, too, had been pumping out monster stories for Atlas, and when that company became Marvel, he was selected by Lee to draw Spider-Man, beginning with the very first story in *Amazing Fantasy* #15. Ditko's art style was, shall we say, unique — it had a looser, sketchier look, with plenty of fine-line detail. Ditko had spent time working for Joe Simon and Jack Kirby's studio in the 1950s, where veteran artist Mort Meskin took him under his wing; Meskin's way with strong layouts and fine-line, clutter-free detail made a big impression on the young artist.

The concept of Spider-Man came from Lee and Kirby, the artist originally tagged to draw this new hero; however, Kirby's sample pages were "too heroic" according to Lee. Ditko was an inspired second choice, and his sometimes frail-looking Peter Parker was perfect for what

Fantastic Four #4 (Marvel, 5/61); Curator pedigree copy, CGC NM+ 9.6, sold for $44,812 in 2012.

Lee had in mind — a typical nerdish, brainy teenager who just happened to be bitten by a radioactively charged spider at a science exhibit. Ditko worked out all the major details for Spider-Man's costume and web-producing wristband. The full-face mask was a bit of a departure for standard comic book heroes, but it worked well with the thin, average-looking Peter Parker. Ditko's design was clearly a winner, and Stan Lee knew he had what he wanted. Steve Ditko would remain the primary artist for not only Spider-Man, but also Marvel's most surreal, mysterious, and cosmic hero, Doctor Strange, until he left Marvel in 1966.

FANTASTIC FOUR, 1961-64

Fantastic Four #12 (Marvel, 3/63); CGC NM+ 9.6, sold for $65,725 in 2012.

▶ Fantastic Four #9 (Marvel, 12/62); CGC NM+ 9.6, sold for $11,352 in 2016.

Fantastic Four Annual #1 (Marvel, 1963); CGC NM+ 9.6, sold for $7,170 in 2016.

Fantastic Four issue #19 (Marvel, 10/63); Pacific Coast pedigree copy, CGC NM+ 9.6, sold for $5,377 in 2012.

Fantastic Four #24 (Marvel, 3/64); Curator pedigree copy, CGC NM+ 9.6, sold for $2,151 in 2012.

Fantastic Four #32 (Marvel, 11/64); CGC NM+ 9.6, sold for $2,270 in 2015.

Fantastic Four #29 (Marvel, 8/64); CGC NM+ 9.6, sold for $7,170 in 2015.

THE VULTURE LOOKS TOO SURE OF HIMSELF! HE MUST HAVE A FOOL-PROOF PLAN TO DEFEAT ME! BUT--WHAT CAN IT *BE*?

HERE IS SPIDER-MAN AS YOU LIKE HIM... FIGHTING! JOKING! DARING! CHALLENGING THE MOST DANGEROUS FOE OF ALL, IN THIS-- THE MARVEL AGE OF COMICS!

Amazing Spider-Man #8 (Marvel, 1/64); CGC NM/MT 9.8, sold for $16,730 in 2012.

Amazing Spider-Man #7 (Marvel, 12/63); Twin Cities pedigree copy, CGC NM+ 9.6, sold for $21,510 in 2014.

Amazing Spider-Man #10 (Marvel, 3/64); Twin Cities pedigree copy, CGC NM/MT 9.8, sold for 15,535 in 2014.

Amazing Spider-Man #15 (Marvel, 8/64); CGC NM+ 9.6, sold for $7,468 in 2015.

Amazing Spider-Man Annual #1 (Marvel, 1964); CGC NM 9.4, sold for $6,000 in 2013.

Amazing Spider-Man #17 (Marvel, 10/64); CGC NM+ 9.6, sold for $5,975 in 2016.

TALES TO ASTONISH: THE HULK AND ANT-MAN/GIANT MAN

Tales to Astonish #59 (Marvel, 9/64); CGC NM+ 9.6, sold for $2,152 in 2016.

Tales to Astonish #27 first appearance of Ant-Man (Marvel, 1/62); CGC VF- 7.5, sold for $11,950 in 2014.

Tales to Astonish #62 (Marvel, 12/64); Twin Cities pedigree copy, CGC NM+ 9.6, sold for $985 in 2011.

Tales to Astonish #35 (Marvel, 9/62); CGC NM- 9.2, sold for $23,900 in 2016.

Tales to Astonish #44 (Marvel, 6/63); CBCS NM 9.4, sold for $6,572 in 2015.

BIG-SCREEN SUPERHEROES

ANT-MAN'S CINEMATIC DEBUT

Marvel Studios/Walt Disney Studios Motion Pictures/Heritage Auctions

As part of expanding its cinematic universe, Marvel called Ant-Man up to the big leagues of the big screen in 2015's *Ant-Man*.

Striking a lighter tone than many of Marvel's other superhero movies, and with comedian Paul Rudd in the title role, *Ant-Man* earned $519.3 million USD at the box office.

The success of this movie has led to a sequel, *Ant-Man and the Wasp* (with Rudd and Evangeline Lily reprising these roles from the first movie), hitting theaters in July. On a side note, this is the first Marvel superhero movie with a female character's name in the title.

JOURNEY iNTO MYSTERY: THOR

▲ Original pin-up page artwork from *Journey Into Mystery* #110 (Marvel, 11/64) by Jack Kirby and Chic Stone; sold for $44,812 in 2011.

Journey into Mystery #84 (Marvel, 9/62); CGC NM 9.4, sold for $35,850 in 2012.

◀ *Journey into Mystery* #89 (Marvel, 2/63); CGC NM 9.4, sold for $9,560 in 2015.

▶ *Journey into Mystery* #100 (Marvel, 1/64); CGC NM 9.4, sold for $1,673 in 2014.

STRANGE TALES: DR. STRANGE AND HUMAN TORCH

Strange Tales #118 (Marvel, 3/64); Northland pedigree copy, CGC NM/MT 9.8, sold for $5,975 in 2012.

Strange Tales #123 (Marvel, 8/64); CGC NM+ 9.6, sold for $1,314 in 2013.

BIG-SCREEN SUPERHEROES

DOCTOR STRANGE CASTS A SPELL

This mystical superhero got his first feature film in 2016 in *Doctor Strange*. With Benedict Cumberbatch in the title role, the movie made some box office magic for Marvel by earning $677.7 million USD and became another hit for the powerhouse production studio.

Although Marvel hasn't officially announced a second Doctor Strange movie as of this writing, the post-credits sequence suggests that there will be one.

Marvel has, however, confirmed that Cumberbatch will reprise the role in the next Avengers movie, *Avengers: Infinity*, due in April. Cumberbatch's Doctor Strange also appears in *Thor: Ragnarok*.

Strange Tales #105 (Marvel, 2/63); Don and Maggie Thompson pedigree copy, CGC NM 9.4, sold for $1,314 in 2014.

Strange Tales #101 (Marvel, 10/62), Human Torch stories begin; CGC NM 9.4, sold for $8,365 in 2016.

Strange Tales #107 (Marvel, 4/62); CGC NM+ 9.6, sold for $5,497 in 2016.

CAPTAIN AMERICA, 1963-64

◄ *The Avengers* #4 (Marvel, 3/64); first "true" Silver Age appearance of Captain America, Pacific Coast pedigree copy, CGC NM+ 9.6, sold for $50,787 in 2012.

Sgt. Fury and His Howling Commandos #13 (Marvel, 12/64); Don and Maggie Thompson pedigree copy, CGC NM+ 9.6, sold for $4,481 in 2013.

Tales of Suspense #58 (Marvel, 10/64); Don and Maggie Thompson pedigree copy, CGC NM 9.4, sold for $3,583 in 2014.

Tales of Suspense #59 (Marvel, 11/64); Pacific Coast pedigree copy, CGC NM/MT 9.8, sold for $6,871 in 2012.

◀ *The Avengers* #1 (Marvel, 9/63); CGC NM+ 9.6, sold for $215,100 in 2015.

The Avengers #11 (Marvel, 12/64); CGC NM 9.4, sold for $1,673 in 2015.

◀ *The Avengers* #3 (Marvel, 1/64); Twin Cities pedigree copy, CGC NM 9.4, sold for $7,468 in 2011.

▶ *The Avengers* #7 (Marvel, 8/64); Don and Maggie Thompson pedigree, CGC NM 9.4, sold for $2,868 in 2013.

Iron Man #54 (Marvel, 6/64); CGC NM+ 9.6, sold for $4,513 in 2016.

Iron Man #43 (Marvel, 7/63); Twin Cities pedigree, CGC NM 9.4, sold for $3,883 in 2011.

Iron Man #56 (Marvel, 8/64); CGC NM+ 9.6, sold for $1,254 in 2016.

X-Men #2 (Marvel, 11/63); Pacific Coast pedigree copy, CGC NM/MT 9.8, sold for $43,318 in 2012.

X-Men #8 (Marvel, 11/64); Pacific Coast pedigree copy, CGC NM/MT 9.8, sold for $7,767 in 2012.

DAREDEVIL, 1964

▶ Original page 20 art from *Daredevil* #5 by Wally Wood; sold for $15,535 in 2013.

Daredevil #2 (Marvel, 6/64); Pacific Coast pedigree copy, CGC NM/MT 9.8, sold for $26,290.00 in 2012.

▶ *Daredevil* #5 (Marvel, 12/64); CGC NM 9.4, sold for $1,015 in 2011.

BIG-SCREEN SUPERHEROES

DAREDEVIL A BIGGER HIT ON TV

Although the 2003 *Daredevil* movie earned $179.2 million at the box office, it is considered by many to be a bust (even Ben Affleck, who played the superhero, once told *Playboy* magazine he regrets making the movie).

But the "man without fear" is having much better success on the small screen. Making its debut on Netflix in 2015, "Daredevil" is the first Marvel original series and has been renewed for a third season. The show follows Matt Murdock (Charlie Cox), attorney by day and vigilante by night. Blinded in an accident as a child, Murdock uses his heightened senses as Daredevil to fight crime on the streets of New York after the sun goes down. While Murdock's day job requires him to believe in the criminal justice system, his alter ego does not follow suit, leading him to take the law into his own hands to protect his Hell's Kitchen neighborhood and the surrounding communities.

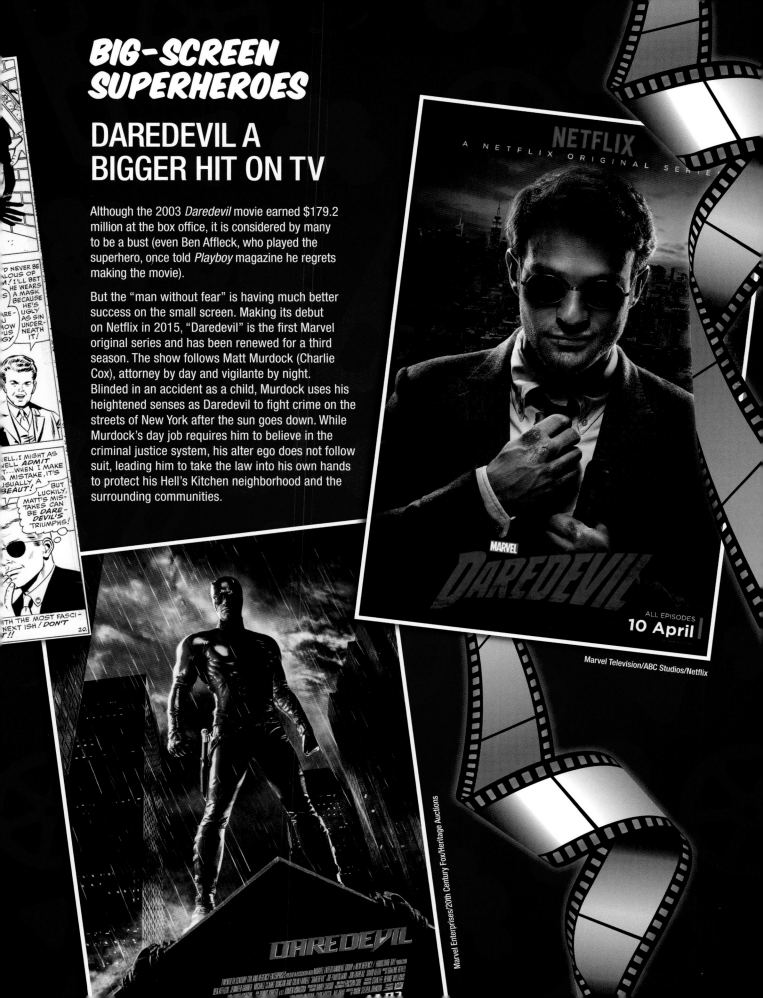

NETFLIX
A NETFLIX ORIGINAL SERIES

MARVEL
DAREDEVIL

ALL EPISODES
10 April

Marvel Television/ABC Studios/Netflix

Marvel Enterprises/20th Century Fox/Heritage Auctions

DAREDEVIL

▼ The Incredible Hulk #2 (Marvel, 7/62); CBCS NM- 9.2, sold for $9,858 in 2015.

The Incredible Hulk #3 (Marvel, 9/62); Don and Maggie Thompson pedigree copy, CGC NM 9.4, sold for $13,742 in 2015.

▶ The Incredible Hulk #5 (Marvel, 1/63); CGC NM- 9.2, sold for $4,541 in 2016.

BIG-SCREEN SUPERHEROES

HULK'S POP-CULTURE SUCCESS

The Incredible Hulk has had his share of pop-culture success, first bursting onto living room TVs in 1978, followed by big-screen solo features in 2003 and 2008.

Executive producer Kenneth Johnson told *Rolling Stone* magazine in 2015 that when creating a TV show about The Incredible Hulk, he borrowed the fugitive concept from *Les Miserables* and a little from *Dr. Jekyll and Mr. Hyde* and decided to make it more of an adult drama built into the traditions of Greek tragedy. That concept may sound kooky for a giant green monster from comic books, but Johnson's vision was a hit.

Centering around widowed scientist Dr. David Banner (Bill Bixby), caught in the middle of an experiment gone bad that makes him transmogrify into a big green monster (Lou Ferrigno) whenever he gets angry, *The Incredible Hulk* ran on CBS for five seasons, from 1978-1982. It was a harbinger of the multimedia domination Marvel Comics' characters would achieve decades later and still have today. The show was a ratings hit and is remembered as one of the best TV shows to come out of the late 1970s/early '80s. Although the show ended in 1982, it remained popular enough to warrant three made-for-TV movies: *Return of the Incredible Hulk* (1988), *Trial of the Incredible Hulk* (1989), and *Death of the The Incredible Hulk* (1990).

More than 20 years later, The Hulk moved to the big screen in 2003's *Hulk*, directed by Ang Lee, and with Eric Bana as the superhero. The movie grossed $245.4 million. Marvel did a second movie in 2008, *The Incredible Hulk*, with Edward Norton as the titular character this time, and directed by Louis Leterrier. It earned $263.4 million. Although both films doubled their budget in ticket sales, and received about the same amount of critical acclaim, the latter movie has been more popular with audiences, according to Rotten Tomatoes.

Today, The Hulk makes appearances in the *Avenger* movies and is played by Mark Ruffalo.

Holy rarity, Batman! This Fillmore Auditorium concert poster BG-2 (Bill Graham, 1966) is without a doubt one of the toughest to find in first printing state. This Big Brother and the Holding Company/Quicksilver Messenger Service concept poster, the second in the Bill Graham Presents series, measures approximately 14" x 19-3/4" and is in Near Mint restored condition. Artist Wes Wilson hand-signed the poster in the lower right corner. It sold at auction for $10,000.

CHAPTER 4

THE POP ART YEARS: 1964-67

THE MiD-1960S were like an explosion of vivid color in America. Comic books were hip again, thanks to high school and college-age kids who were buying Marvel. Pop music was peaking with The Beatles and other "British Invasion" bands like The Rolling Stones, Dave Clark Five, and The Animals. Fine art made a drastic turn to the left with a number of artists inspired by pop culture in general and comic books in particular, with canvases by Andy Warhol, Roy Lichtenstein, Mel Ramos, and others commanding huge prices. Suddenly, superhero comic books were "camp," where outrageous storylines, costumes, and villains were celebrated as being "so bad they're good" by the mainstream. For kids like me who seriously read and collected comics, "camp" was a bit of an embarrassment, but welcomed nonetheless for the positive attention the comics were receiving. For a while, it seemed everyone wanted to jump on the superhero bandwagon, and costumed crime-fighters were everywhere.

By 1965, superhero comics began to reflect the pop-minded attitude of the country. The Beatles made their way into the comics world. *Strange Tales* #130 (March 1965) had the bizarre sight of the Fantastic Four's Human Torch and Thing in "Beatle Wigs," and in the story titled "Meet the Beatles!" where Ben (Thing) and Johnny (Human Torch) take dates to a Beatles concert.

BATMAN GETS A MAKEOVER

In 1964, an important change was taking place with one of DC's best-known characters. For years, Batman's popularity had been sliding,

Batman and Robin screen print, from a painting by Mel Ramos; sold for $4,375 in 2013.

and the look of the feature played a part. Artist Sheldon Moldoff had been chosen in the late 1950s to be the new "Bob Kane" (the creator of Batman had a clause in his contract that insured his name would remain on the feature, years after he stopped handling the art chores). Moldoff was a competent artist who had worked for DC since the early Golden Age, but his Batman looked stiff, especially when compared to the dynamic (if somewhat cartoony) designs of chief 1950s artist Dick Sprang, or the photo-realism of Curt Swan. When Julie Schwartz became editor of the Batman titles, he teamed with "Flash" artist Carmine Infantino to develop a new, more realistic art style and story approach to depicting the Caped Crusader; his sleek version debuted in *Detective Comics* #327 (May 1964), and continued on with *Batman* #164 (June 1964). The contrast between this issue's "New Look" Batman with the issue before (#326, with the cover story "Captives of the Alien Zoo") were startling to the few old-time fans of the series, but much more appealing to newer readers. The "New Look" introduced Batman's yellow oval around the bat emblem on his costume, where it would remain for the next twenty years.

Also added to the Batman mix was a shift from the sci-fi stories of the past few years, with a new focus on actual detective work for Batman and Robin, including the return of the Joker and a few more of the Gotham Guardian's more colorful foes. A real surprise was the second coming of the Riddler, a character that had been used only twice in the 1940s (*Detective Comics* #140 and #142, both from 1948). The Riddler was featured in the *Batman* #171 (May 1965) cover story, "Remarkable Ruse of the Riddler!"

Side note: In 1965, television producer William Dozier was at the airport, about to catch a flight from New York to Los Angeles, when he spotted *Batman* #171, with Batman and Robin spinning the Riddler around like a top. Dozier supposedly had never read a comic book before, but Batman was one of several comic-related characters under consideration by ABC for a new series, and this issue grabbed his attention. Something big was about to happen!

BATMAN BECOMES A TV STAR

Without a doubt, the biggest "Pop Art" event occurred on January 12, 1966. That's when ABC's *Batman* series premiered, starring Adam West as Batman/Bruce Wayne, with Burt Ward as Robin/Dick Grayson. The series borrowed heavily for the recent "New Look" comic book storylines; in fact, the first two-part story, "Hi Diddle Riddle/Smack in the Middle," was based

Batman #171 (DC, 5/65), first Silver Age Riddler appearance; Twin Cities pedigree copy, CGC NM+ 9.6, sold for $13,132 in 2011.

largely on that issue of *Batman* Mr. Dozier had picked up at the airport, featuring the Riddler. However, the tone of the series was nowhere near as straight-faced as the comic books they emulated; Dozier has been quoted as saying, "I had the simple idea of overdoing it, of making it so square and so serious that adults would find it amusing." The kids, he figured, would just be happy to see their heroes on TV and not question the over-the-top nature of the writing. The series also borrowed the "cliffhanger" approach used in movie serials of the 1930s-50s, with an urging to "tune in tomorrow – same Bat-time, same Bat-channel" at the end of the Wednesday night half-hour, for the concluding part of the story shown on Thursdays.

The *Batman* TV series was a big, immediate hit that everyone at the time talked about. Seemingly overnight, the entire country was mad for superhero comic books, and anything

A 1966 *New York TV Magazine* with Adam West as Batman photo cover; sold for $19 in 2007.

'BATMAN' HELPS BAD MEN MAKE GOOD

WHERE WAS i?

WHEN THAT FiRST EPiSODE of *Batman* aired on ABC-TV, I was right there, glued to my set. Batman had been my "first love," comic book-wise, but the "New Look" didn't appeal that much to me – I preferred those sillier, sci-fi-tinged stories of the early sixties. By this time, I was mostly picking up just the 80-page Giant issues, reveling in those "old-school" stories featuring Batman without that annoying yellow oval on his chest. I wasn't picking up very many Marvels during this time – it took me a few years to fully get into the Stan Lee method of comic storytelling. Hey, I was just a kid!

connected to them. There were promotional tie-ins with dairies, cereal companies, and about a zillion toy manufacturers, who immediately began flooding the market with all manner of Bat-toys. The show, with its splashy "Zing! Pow!" visuals and corny catchphrases like "Holy Ashtray" were at first met with utter delight by all but the most dedicated comic book fans, who saw through all the color and hype. And the villains – Riddler, The Joker, The Penguin, The Mad Hatter, and (most famously) Catwoman – made the leap from the four-color printed page to the small screen, with some characters played by multiple actors throughout the show's three-year run.

Some bad guys were developed just for the show, designed around whatever guest star was lined up to appear. For a while, it seemed every half-forgotten Hollywood star was lobbying for a guest spot. Among the parade of familiar faces was Frank Gorshin (Riddler, later played by John Astin), Cesar Romero (Joker), Burgess Meredith (Penguin), Julie Newmar (super-slinky Catwoman, later portrayed by Eartha Kitt, and in a feature-length movie, Lee Merriweather); David Wayne (Mad Hatter); Victor Buono (a wonderfully cheesy King Tut, developed just for the show); Roddy McDowall (Bookworm, another villain unique to the series); and Vincent Price (Egghead). As the series grew in popularity, the guest list was bumped up with such notables as Van Johnson, Art Carney, Shelly Winters, Anne Baxter, Eli Wallach (one of three actors to play Mr. Freeze, along with Otto Preminger, and George Sanders), Walter Slezak, Carolyn Jones, Cliff Robertson, Michael Rennie, Tallulah Bankhead, Joan Collins, Ethel Merman, Milton Berle, Anne Baxter, Rudy Vallee, Ida Lupino, Zsa Zsa Gabor, even Liberace – and there were others.

Batman Toothbrush (Butler), sold for $262 in 2016.

To Joe – Best Wishes from Murphy Anderson

▲ This Batman and Robin original artwork, part of a series of 1966 Batman pin-up posters by Carmine Infantino and Murphy Anderson, sold for $28,750 in 2002.

◄ Batman Spring Wound Ride On Batmobile (Marx), sold for $418 in 2011.

Batman Board Game (Milton Bradley), sold for $42 in 2011.

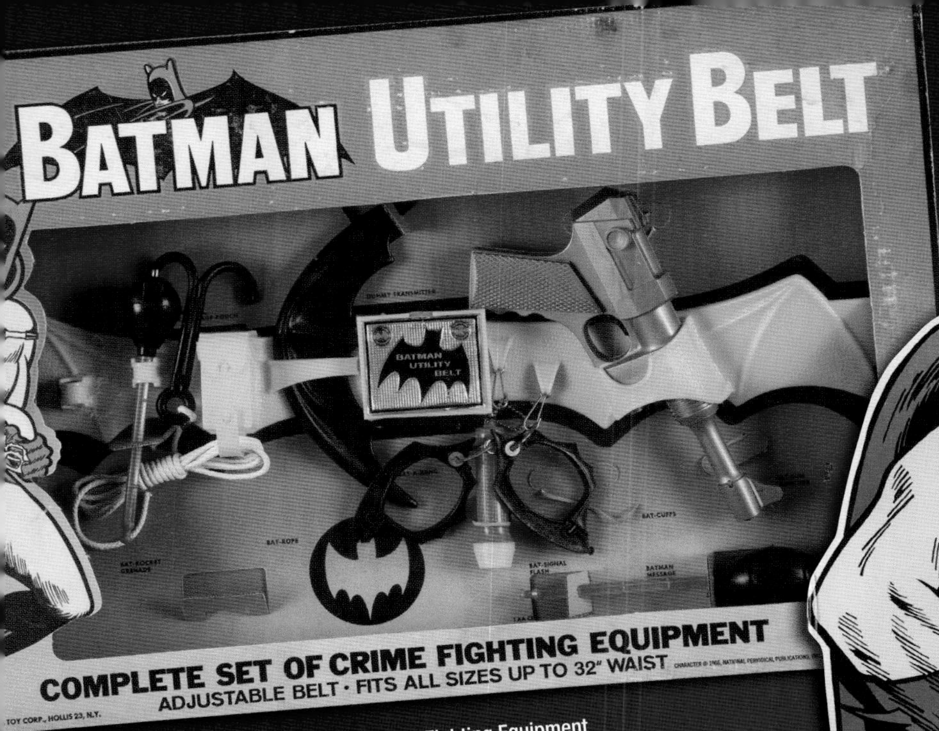
BATMAN UTILITY BELT
BATMAN UTILITY BELT
COMPLETE SET OF CRIME FIGHTING EQUIPMENT
ADJUSTABLE BELT · FITS ALL SIZES UP TO 32" WAIST

Batman Utility Belt Crime Fighting Equipment Playset (Ideal), sold for $5,676 in 2012.

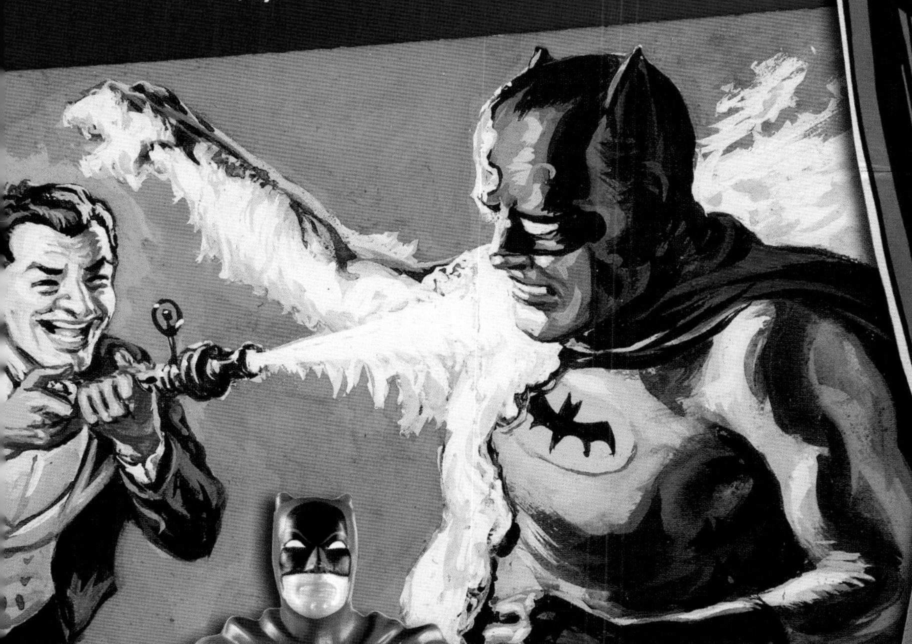

▲ Original art for a 1966 Batman trading card by Norman Saunders; sold for $4,481 in 2009.

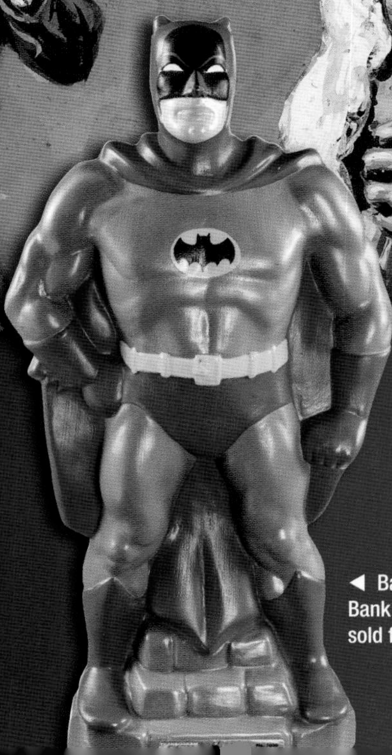

◀ Batman Plastic Bank (Transogram), sold for $155 in 2016.

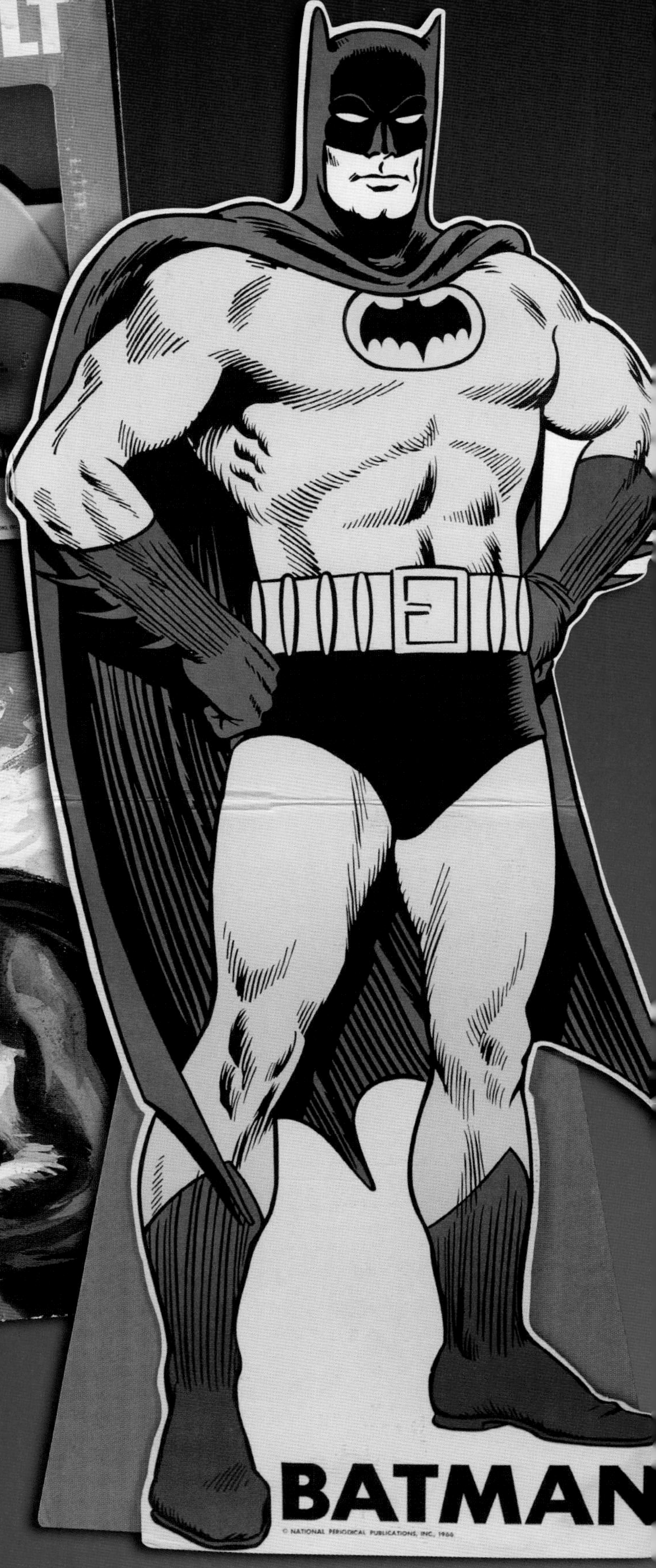
BATMAN

Batman 6-foot Cardboard Standee (All Star Dairies/DC), sold for $1,015 in 2007.

Original artwork for a series of Batman pin-up posters by Carmine Infantino and Murphy Anderson: The Joker, sold for $26,290 in 2016; The Penguin, sold for $15,535 in 2016; The Riddler, sold for $22,705 in 2016.

BATMAN'S GREATEST NEMESIS

Batman is famous for his gallery of villainous rogues, but the one who will always be his greatest nemesis is The Joker, who has been tormenting him since 1940. The Joker has been an enduring pop-culture character still making his mark in the Batman movie franchise, and has been portrayed over the years by a variety of actors, who have each made him their own.

Cesar Romero, *Batman* **(1966):** Cesar Romero's Joker was the first to bust out of the comic books. With his deranged cackle, eyes a poppin', and theatrical pizzazz, his performance set the standard for other Jokers to come.

20th Century Fox Television/Warner Bros. Television Distribution/ABC

Warner Bros. Pictures

Jack Nicholson, *Batman* **(1989):** You might be hard-pressed to find anyone who thinks any actor other than Jack Nicholson should have been cast as The Joker, and who would disagree that he stole this movie with his over-the-top and exuberant performance. As the first "movie" Joker, Nicholson introduced the maniacal villain to mainstream audiences and a new generation of fans. Nicholson instilled his Joker with a wacky outlandishness, and a much darker spin.

Heath Ledger, *The Dark Knight* (2008):
Ledger's bold turn as The Joker revels in the
sheer fun of sadism. What makes his performance
visionary and hilarious (and scary) is the way he
shows us the damage behind the manic giggle
and insanity. Ledger made evil into something
mesmerizing and timeless, and his Joker is
considered the definitive by many fans and critics.

Legendary Pictures/Syncopy/Warner Bros. Pictures

DC Entertainment/Warner Bros. Pictures

Jared Leto, *Suicide Squad* (2016): Leto's
Joker, with dead eyes and a mouth full of silver-
capped teeth, turns his menacingly-switched-
on-and-off smile into a full-metal grimace.
He's the most coldly homicidal of all Jokers and
gives a steely and energetic performance.

MARVEL EXPLORES NEW FRONTIERS

During this time, Marvel was really forging
ahead into new territories with inventive
storylines that ran two or three issues, with
overlapping details from one title to another. The
Doctor Strange stories appearing in *Strange Tales*
were some of the most psychedelic comics of
the decade, with fantastic, cosmos-spanning art
by Steve Ditko. The Hulk had lost his own title
after *The Incredible Hulk* #6, but the green goliath
wasted little time rebounding, with stories
appearing in *Tales to Astonish*, beginning with a
guest shot in an Ant-Man story (*Tales to Astonish*
#59, September 1964). He became a regular
feature with the next issue, sharing honors with
Ant-Man/Giant-Man.

With *Tales to Astonish* #70 (August 1965),
Sub-Mariner took over the Giant-Man spot;
Subby and Hulk manned the title for the
remainder of its run, which ended with #101
(March 1968).

Iron Man ruled the roost over at *Tales of*
Suspense, where he had been introduced with
issue #39 (March 1963). He would share the title
with Captain America, beginning with issue #59
(November 1964).

Marvel's most mysterious hero rode into the
picture on a gleaming surfboard, in *Fantastic Four*
#48 (March 1966), which kicked off a three-
issue storyline introducing The Silver Surfer and
Galactus. The Silver Surfer seems now to be
an obvious cash-in to California's surfing craze,
as seen in all those beach movies with Frankie
Avalon and Annette Funicello, but for the kids
back then (most of whom were too young to
actually surf), this was exciting. The notion of
cruising through the galaxy on a silver surfboard
was heady stuff, to be sure. The Silver Surfer
would guest star several times with the FF before
getting his own title in 1968.

It's odd to think of The X-Men today as a
second-rate superhero team, but that's how many
during the sixties viewed them. Still, their comic
book hung in there long enough for a reboot in
1975, one that would make them one of Marvel's

Both Marvel and DC sought to "dress up" their respective publications with some sort of notice that you would be entering into "camp" territory whenever you picked up a copy. For Marvel, the phrase "Marvel Pop Art Productions" was added to a few covers of comics dated September through December 1965. By March 1966, this had been replaced with "Marvel Comics Group" in big display lettering along the top left corner of each cover. For DC, a checkerboard top edge was added to covers beginning with March 1966 titles; these "go-go checks" (as they were referred to in letter columns and house ads) continued until mid-1967. By then, the novelty wore off. The *Batman* TV series limped through a third season (reduced to only one episode per week), as the jokes grew stale and the plotlines grew increasingly more ridiculous and unbelievable. The bloom was off the rose for campy superheroes. It was time to get back to basics.

Original artwork from *Fantastic Four* #55 featuring The Silver Surfer, by Jack Kirby and Joe Sinnott; sold for $155,350 in 2012.

▶ *Amazing Spider-Man* #39 (Marvel, 8/66), first issue with art by John Romita Sr.; CGC NM/MT 9.8, sold for $13,145 in 2011.

most popular franchises ever. The Avengers fared much better during this time as a strong seller with lots of cool characters and storylines (and of course, that snappy Stan Lee patter that made Marvel the number one choice with all the "hip" kids).

The *Amazing Spider-Man* comic shifted gears in a dramatic fashion with issue #39 (August 1966). Artist Steve Ditko was out, and his quirky but endearing art style was replaced with the more conventional work of John Romita. For some readers (like me), this change was unacceptable, but for many others, it opened the door wide with Romita's clean, easy-to-follow line work. Romita's comic art soon exemplified the Marvel House Style for the rest of the decade.

POP CULTURE EVENTS, 1964-67

APRIL 1965 . . . . . . The Astrodome opens in Houston, Texas

MAY 1965 . . . . The first skateboard championship is held

JUNE 1965 . . . . . . Astronaut Edward Higgins White makes the first U.S. spacewalk

JULY 1965 . . . . Bob Dylan stuns his fans by going electric at the Newport Folk Festival; The second Beatles movie, *Help!,* premieres

DECEMBER 1965 . . . The first Peanuts TV special, *A Charlie Brown Christmas,* debuts on CBS

JULY 1966 . . . . Bob Dylan retreats to his Woodstock, NY, home after a motorcycle accident

AUGUST 1966 . . . . . "Light My Fire," first single by The Doors, is released; The Beatles play their last concert at Candlestick Park, San Francisco

SEPTEMBER 1966 . . *Star Trek* premieres on NBC-TV

DECEMBER 1966 . . . Walt Disney dies; *How the Grinch Stole Christmas* premieres on CBS-TV

JANUARY 1967 . . . . Ronald Reagan becomes governor of California; the Human Be-In is held in San Francisco; astronauts Gus Grissom, Edward Higgins White, and Roger Chaffee are killed when a fire breaks out inside their Apollo spacecraft during a test

MAY 1967 . . . . The Jimi Hendrix Experience release their first album, *Are You Experienced*

JUNE 1967 . . . . The Beatles release the classic album *Sgt. Pepper's Lonely Hearts Club;* "Summer of Love" begins in San Francisco; Monterey Pop Festival three-day event is held

William Shatner as Captain James T. Kirk and Leonard Nimoy as Spock in *Star Trek.* Desilu Productions/Paramount Television/NBC

AUGUST 1967 . . . . . The first album by psychedelic pioneers Pink Floyd is released in the UK; Beatles manager Brian Epstein dies; the final episode of *The Fugitive* airs on ABC-TV, attracting 78 million viewers

OCTOBER 1967 . . . . The musical play "Hair" opens off-Broadway; *The Jungle Book,* the last film supervised by Walt Disney, opens

BATMAN THE BIGGEST SUPERHERO MOVIE FRANCHISE

Tim Burton is credited with starting the superhero genre with his 1989 movie, *Batman*. Burton's inspired take on The Caped Crusader proved that audiences could take comic-book characters seriously and the movie was the start of a blockbuster franchise that, to date, has earned $3.4 billion at the Box Office domestically.

After Burton's successful sequel, *Batman Returns*, the franchise saw a couple of clunkers (Joel Schumacher's *Batman Forever* and *Batman & Robin*, which he has apologized for), until Christopher Nolan resuscitated it with *The Dark Knight* in 2008 and subsequent sequels.

In all, Batman has 11 different movies under its cape that have propelled it as the top-grossing superhero franchise. According to stats at boxofficemojo.com (inflation-adjusted), here is how the movies stack up:

Warner Bros. Pictures

2. *Batman* (1989), total grossed: **$556,518,800**

Legendary Pictures/Syncopy/Warner Bros. Pictures

3. *The Dark Knighr Rises* (2012), total grossed: **$509,023, 200**

Warner Bros. Pictures

4. *Batman Forever* (1995), total grossed: **$373,985,100**

Warner Bros. Pictures

5. *Batman Returns* (1992), total grossed: **$346,851,100**

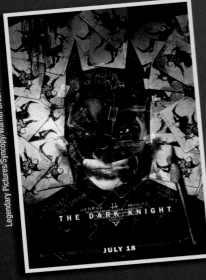

Legendary Pictures/Syncopy/Warner Bros. Pictures

1. *The Dark Knight* (2008), total grossed: **$656,538,100**

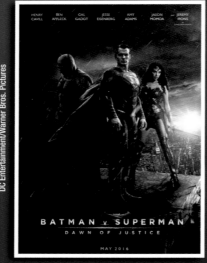

DC Entertainment/Warner Bros. Pictures

6. *Batman V Superman: Dawn of Justice* (2016), total grossed: **$338, 224, 000**

7. *Batman Begins* (2005). total grossed: **$283,188,600**

8. *Batman & Robin* (1997), total grossed: **$206,700,400**

9. *The LEGO Batman Movie* (2017), total grossed: **$175,750,400**

10. *Batman: Mask of the Phantasm* (1993), total grossed: **$11,940,800**

11. *Batman: The Killing Joke* (2017), total grossed: **$3,921,400**

VARIOUS ACTORS HAVE INTERPRETED THE DARK KNIGHT

Pop-culture icon Adam West had exclusivity to the Bat Cape for more than 20 years, but here are the other actors who have portrayed the Caped Crusader and his ego Bruce Wayne in the movie franchise:

Warner Bros. Pictures

Warner Bros. Pictures

Warner Bros. Pictures

MICHAEL KEATON: BATMAN (1989) AND BATMAN RETURNS (1992)

Michael Keaton was the first to don the mask in 1989's *Batman*, and his portrayal broke the camp mold of West's, shedding the silliness for something much darker. Keaton's casting was controversial at the time and many fans flipped out over it, writing 50,000 protest letters demanding a re-cast. Keaton nailed it, though, and imbued his Batman with a haunting intensity, and Bruce Wayne with an aura of mystery. His brooding portrayal of Batman set the standard and is considered by many fans and movie critics to be the best.

VAL KILMER: BATMAN FOREVER (1995)

When Keaton decided not to return to the role, Val Kilmer stepped into the cowl. His Bruce Wayne was slick and charming, and his Batman was toned down and lighter than Keaton's. Kilmer's performance is serviceable, if not that memorable.

CHRISTIAN BALE: BATMAN BEGINS (2005), THE DARK KNIGHT (2008), THE DARK KNIGHT RISES (2012)

After a lighter Batman in the previous two movies, Christian Bale made the Dark Knight dark, bringing a new seriousness and gritty vision to the role. Borrowing from the more adult nature of modern *Batman* comics, Bale's performance emphasizes Bruce Wayne's emotional torment, and his Batman is transformed into more of an action hero. Bale's Batman is a hit with many fans, but almost no one can figure out why he chose to give the character an odd guttural voice.

GEORGE CLOONEY: BATMAN & ROBIN (1997)

Clooney's performance as the Caped Crusader was reminiscent of the camp of West. He even once joked that he helped to kill the franchise, which had way more to do with the movie itself - considered the worst in the franchise - than the fact his Batsuit had nipples.

DC Entertainment/Warner Bros. Pictures

BEN AFFLECK: BATMAN V SUPERMAN: DAWN OF JUSTICE (2016), JUSTICE LEAGUE (2017)

Ben Affleck donned the cinematic cape and cowl for the first time in *Batman V Superman: Dawn of Justice*. He, too, faced some initial criticism by fans, but his performance is considered one of the high points of that movie. Affleck channels an older and wiser vision of the character that, perhaps more than anyone, is influenced by the jaded Batman of Frank Miller's *The Dark Knight Returns*.

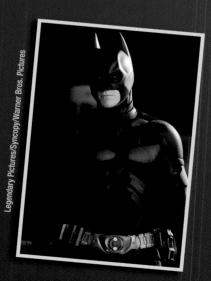
Legendary Pictures/Syncopy/Warner Bros. Pictures

Original cover art for *Superman* #180 by Curt Swan and George Klein; sold for $39,435 in 2009.

Superboy #120 (DC, 4/65); Twin Cities pedigree copy, CGC NM+ 9.6, sold for $1,434 in 2011.

Adventure Comics #333 (DC, 6/65); CGC NM+ 9.6, sold for $1.314 in 2013.

Superman's Girl Friend Lois Lane #54 (DC, 1/65); CGC NM+ 9.6, sold for $155 in 2012.

80 Page Giant #6 (DC, 1/65); CGC NM 9.4, sold for $657 in 2016.

Superman's Pal Jimmy Olsen #88 (DC, 10/65); CGC NM- 9.2, sold for $74 in 2016.

Detective Comics #342 (DC, 8/65); Pacific Coast pedigree copy, CGC NM+ 9.6, sold for $1,374 in 2011.

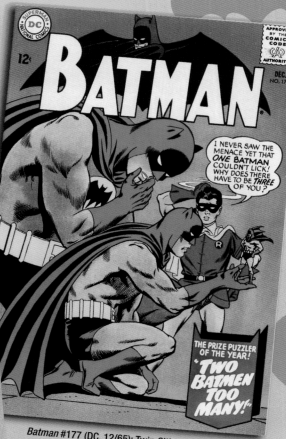

Batman #177 (DC, 12/65); Twin Cities pedigree copy, CGC NM+ 9.6, sold for $836 in 2012.

Batman #174 (DC, 9/65); Boston pedigree copy, CGC NM 9.4, sold for $454 in 2015.

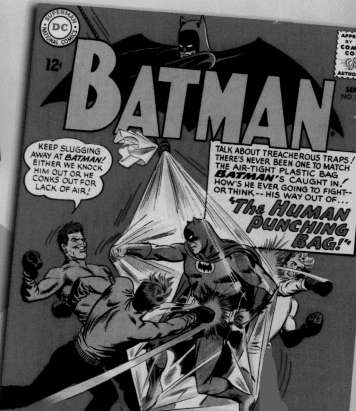

BATMAN iN THE BRAVE AND THE BOLD

▲ Original splash page art by Win Mortimer for *Brave and the Bold* #64; sold for $1,725 in 2005.

▲ *Brave and the Bold* issue #64 (DC, 3/66); Rocky Mountain pedigree copy, CGC NM/MT 9.8, sold for $567 in 2012.

Brave and the Bold issue #68 (DC, 11/66); Pacific Coast pedigree copy, sold for $567 in 2013.

◄ *Action Comics* #344 (DC, 12/66); Twin Cities pedigree copy, CGC NM+ 9.6, sold for $451 in 2016.

Batman #181 (DC, 6/66); CGC NM+ 9.6, sold for $4,481 in 2013.

World's Finest Comics #165 (DC, 3/67); CGC NM+ 9.6, sold for $167 in 2017.

Superman #194 (DC, 2/67); CGC NM 9.4, sold for $262 in 2016.

Original cover art to *World's Finest Comics* #168 by Curt Swan and George Klein, sold for $50,190 in 2016.

Detective Comics #362 (DC, 4/67); Pacific Coast pedigree copy, CGC NM/MT 9.8, sold for $2,629 in 2011.

Green Lantern #52 (DC, 4/67); Oakland pedigree copy, CGC NM+ 9.6, sold for $388 in 2013.

Detective Comics #359 (DC, 1/67); first new Batgirl appearance, CGC NM+ 9.6, sold for $5,377 in 2013.

Batman #183 (DC, 8/66); CGC NM/MT 9.8, sold for $1,912 in 2011.

▲ *Superman #198 (7/67); CGC NM+ 9.6, sold for $334 in 2016.*

◀ *Superman's Girl Friend Lois Lane #68 aka 80 Page Giant #26 (10/66); Twin Cities pedigree copy, CGC NM- 9.2, sold for $185 in 2013.*

▼ *Metal Men #20 (DC, 7/66); CGC NM 9.4, sold for $221 in 2012.*

Wonder Woman #169 (4/67); CGC NM 9.4, sold for $179 in 2017.

Adventure Comics #350 (11/66); Double Cover copy, CGC NM+ 9.6, sold for $478 in 2013.

▲ Aquaman #27 (5-6/66); Savannah pedigree copy, CGC NM- 9.2, sold for $84 in 2011.

◄ Showcase #64 (9-10/66); CGC NM- 9.2, sold for $250 in 2013.

MARVEL 'POP ART' PRODUCTIONS, 1965

Amazing Spider-Man #30 (Marvel, 11/65); CGC NM/MT 9.8, sold for $8,245 in 2011.

Amazing Spider-Man #31 (Marvel, 12/65); Boston pedigree copy, CGC NM+ 9.6, sold for $8,962 in 2016.

◀ *Daredevil* #9 (Marvel, 8/65); CGC NM+ 9.6, sold for $956 in 2015.

▶ *Avengers* #19 (Marvel, 8/65); CGC NM+ 9.6, sold for $896 in 2015.

Original cover art to *Daredevil* #9 by Wally Wood (1965); sold for $149,375 in 2016.

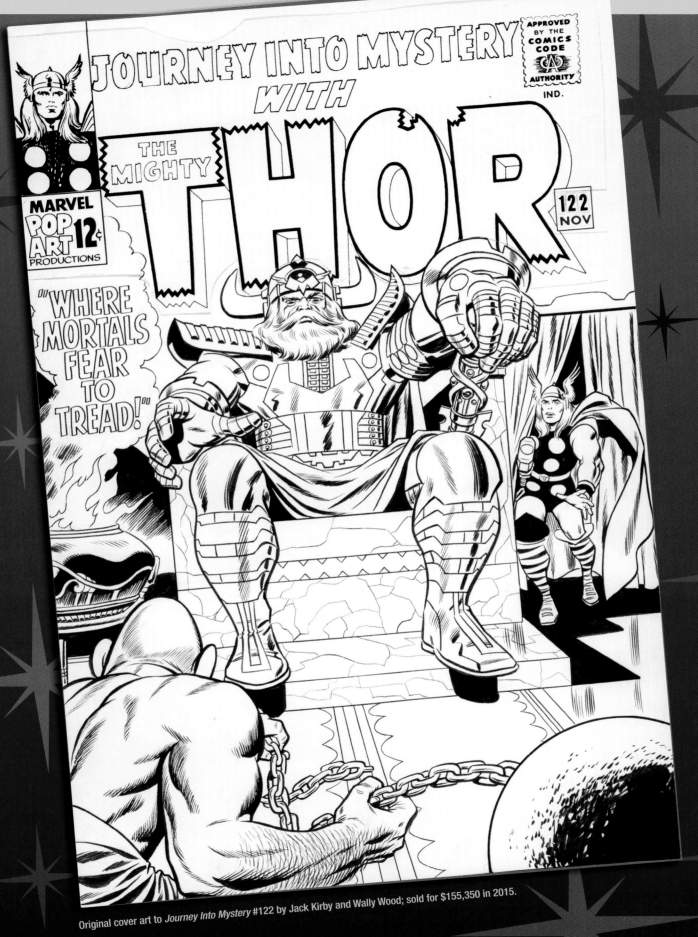

Original cover art to *Journey Into Mystery* #122 by Jack Kirby and Wally Wood; sold for $155,350 in 2015.

MARVEL 'POP ART' PRODUCTIONS, 1965

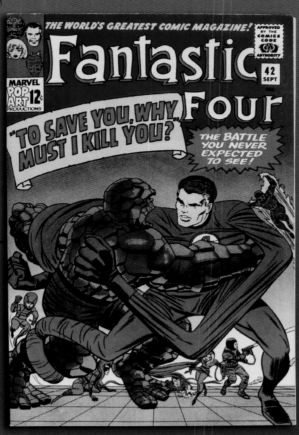

Fantastic Four #42 (Marvel, 9/65); Don/Maggie Thompson pedigree copy, CGC NM+ 9.6, sold for $2,270 in 2014.

▲ Fantastic Four #45 (Marvel, 12/65); CGC NM/MT 9.8, sold for $35,850 in 2016.

▶ X-Men #14 (Marvel, 11/65), Rocky Mountain pedigree copy, CGC NM+ 9.6, sold for $2,629 in 2012.

◀ Journey Into Mystery #120 (Marvel, 9/65); CGC NM 9.4, sold for $717 in 2016.

DOC OCK WINS!

Amazing Spider-Man #55 (Marvel, 12/67); Twin Cities pedigree copy, CGC NM+ 9.6, sold for $896 in 2014.

Amazing Spider-Man #50 (Marvel, 7/67); CGC NM/MT 9.8, sold for $26,290 in 2011.

▶ Amazing Spider-Man #54 (Marvel, 11/67); CGC NM+ 9.6, sold for $896 in 2014.

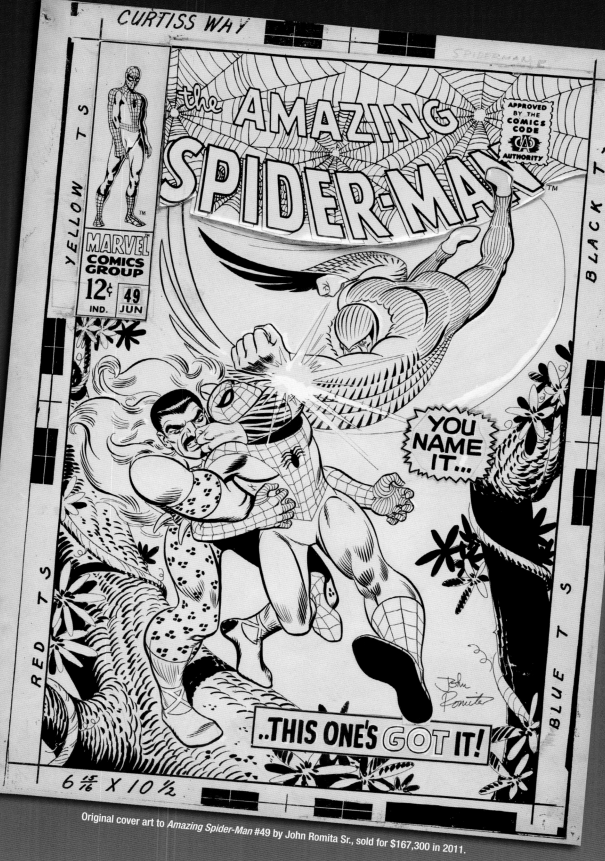

Original cover art to *Amazing Spider-Man #49* by John Romita Sr., sold for $167,300 in 2011.

▶ Fantastic Four #50 (Marvel, 5/66); CGC NM/MT 9.8, sold for $26,290 in 2011.

▲ Fantastic Four #46 (Marvel, 1/66); Northland pedigree copy, CGC NM/MT 9.8, sold for $15,535 in 2015.

▶ Fantastic Four #54 (Marvel, 9/66); CGC NM/MT 9.8, sold for $896 in 2014.

Chadwick Boseman stars as Black Panther.
Marvel Studios/Walt Disney Studios Motion Pictures

Marvel Studios/Walt Disney Studios Motion Pictures

Marvel introduces the first Black Superhero, The Black Panther, in *Fantastic Four* #52 (Marvel, 7/66). CGC NM/MT 9.8, sold for $83,650 in 2016.

BIG-SCREEN SUPERHEROES

BLACK PANTHER STARS IN SOLO MOVIE

After making his big screen debut in 2016's *Captain America: Civil War*, Black Panther finally got his own film in the Marvel Cinematic Universe, which was set to debut on Feb. 16, 2018, after this book went to press.

The Ryan Coogler-directed *Black Panther* will focus on the superhero's homeland of Wakanda, and the star-studded cast includes Chadwick Boseman (T'Challa, a.k.a. Black Panther), Michael B. Jordan (villain Erik Killmonger), Lupita Nyong'o (Nakia) and Forest Whitaker (Zuri).

Fans have waited for years for Black Panther to get his own movie and when the cast appeared at 2017's Comic-Con International to show the trailer, it was met with wild enthusiasm and earned a standing ovation, according to Wired.com.

Unlike previous Marvel movies, which have either been primarily set in New York or space, *Black Panther* takes place in Wakanda, the technologically advanced (and vibranium-rich) African nation. T'Challa is now king of Wakanda following the death of his father. Threats from inside Wakanda and out have little sympathy that he's a newcomer both to the throne and the Avengers; it's time for T'Challa to figure out, in the words of fighter Nakia, "what kind of king [he is] going to be."

Although the movie came out while this book was at the printer, we're betting that it will be a blockbuster and may be another franchise in the making for Marvel.

▼ Daredevil #14 (Marvel, 3/66); CGC NM+ 9.6, sold for $466 in 2013.

▲ Daredevil #10 (Marvel, 10/65); Boston pedigree copy, CGC NM/MT 9.8, sold for $5,377 in 2012.

▶ Tales of Suspense #82 (Marvel, 10/66); Don and Maggie Thompson pedigree copy, CGC NM+ 9.6, sold for $478 in 2014.

▲ Tales of Suspense #74 (Marvel, 2/66); CGC NM 9.4, sold for $143 in 2014.

▲ *Strange Tales* #148 (Marvel, 9/66); CGC NM+ 9.6, sold for $896 in 2016.

◄ *Tales to Astonish* #81 (Marvel, 6/66); CGC NM 9.4, sold for $239 in 2014.

▲ *Tales to Astonish* #93 (Marvel, 7/67); CGC NM/MT 9.8, sold for $13,145 in 2012.

◄ *Strange Tales* #158 (Marvel, 7/67); Pacific Coast pedigree copy, CGC NM/MT 9.8, sold for $985 in 2012.

Original story page art from *The Avengers* #3 featuring the Hulk, by Jack Kirby and Paul Reinman; signed by Jack Kirby. Sold for $5,975 in 2006.

THE AVENGERS, 1965-1967

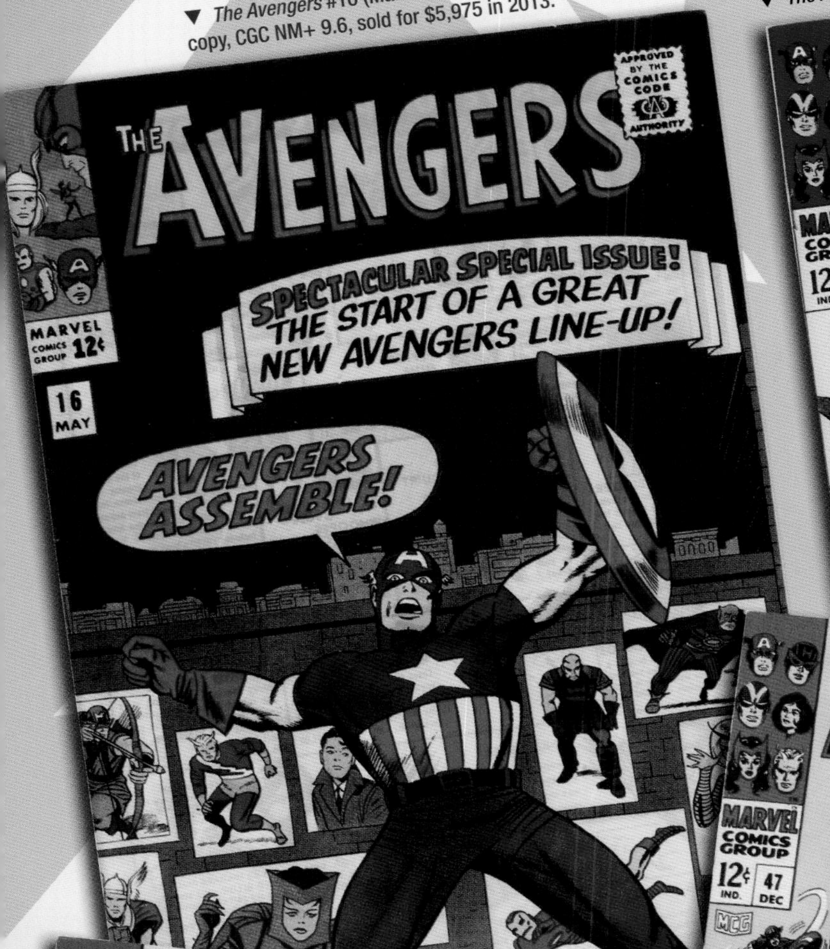

THE AVENGERS
APPROVED BY THE COMICS CODE AUTHORITY
MARVEL COMICS GROUP 12¢
16 MAY
SPECTACULAR SPECIAL ISSUE! THE START OF A GREAT NEW AVENGERS LINE-UP!
AVENGERS ASSEMBLE!

▼ *The Avengers* #16 (Marvel, 5/65); Twin Cities pedigree copy, CGC NM+ 9.6, sold for $5,975 in 2013.

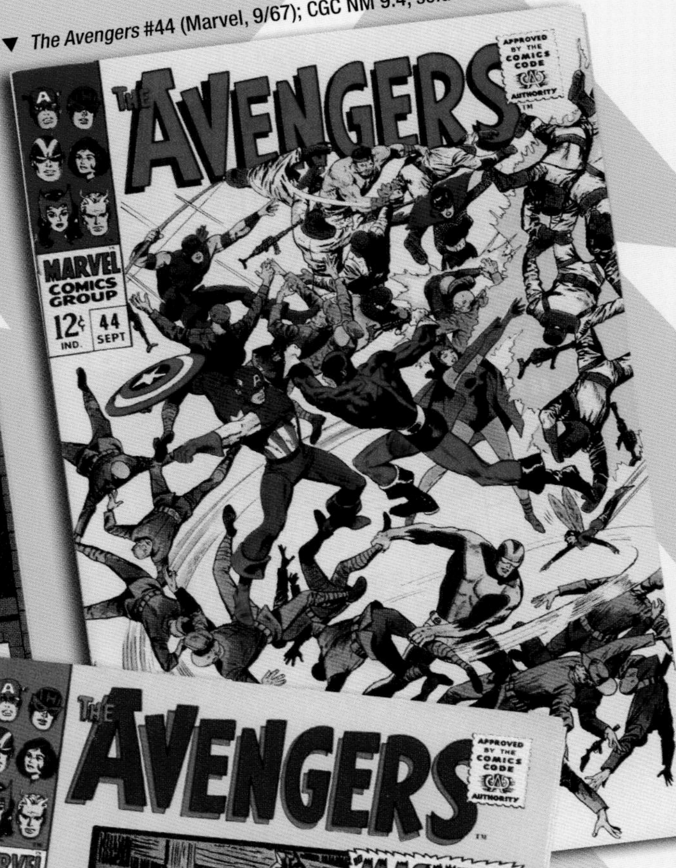

THE AVENGERS
APPROVED BY THE COMICS CODE AUTHORITY
MARVEL COMICS GROUP
12¢ IND. 44 SEPT

▼ *The Avengers* #44 (Marvel, 9/67); CGC NM 9.4, sold for $382 in 2015.

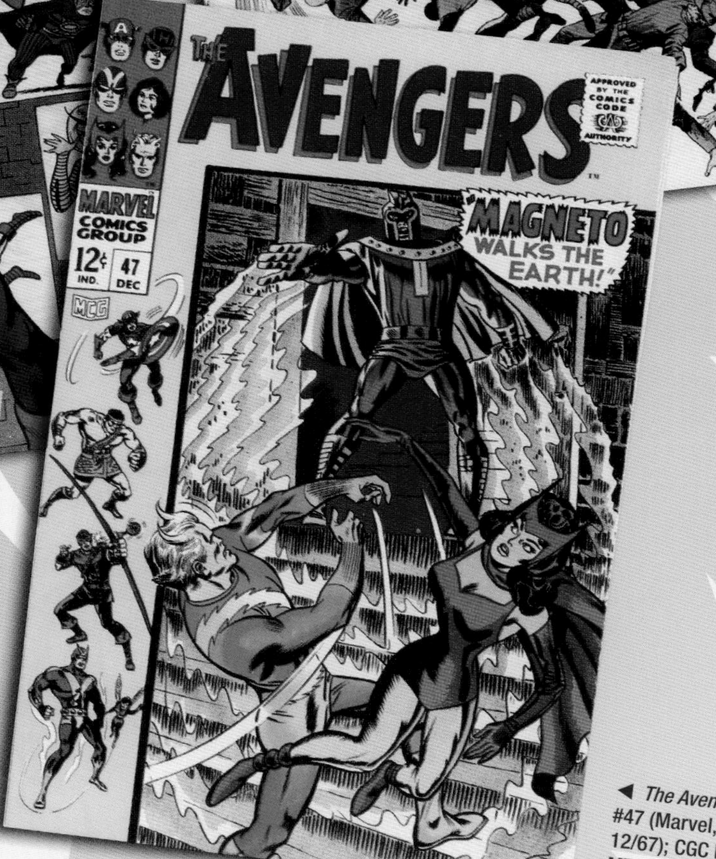

THE AVENGERS
APPROVED BY THE COMICS CODE AUTHORITY
MARVEL COMICS GROUP
12¢ IND. 47 DEC
MCG
"MAGNETO WALKS THE EARTH!"

◀ *The Avengers* #47 (Marvel, 12/67); CGC NM/MT 9.8, sold for $549 in 2017.

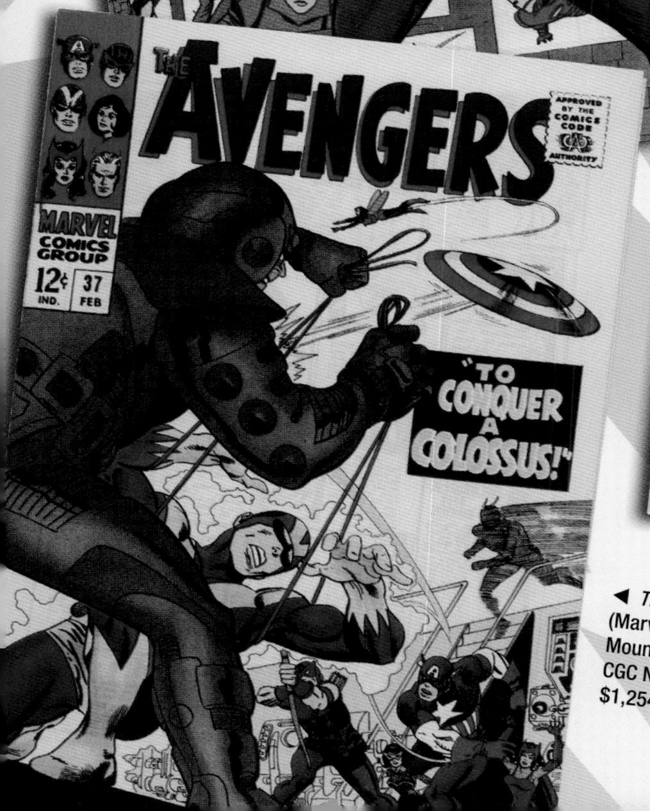

THE AVENGERS
APPROVED BY THE COMICS CODE AUTHORITY
MARVEL COMICS GROUP
12¢ IND. 37 FEB
"TO CONQUER A COLOSSUS!"

◀ *The Avengers* #37 (Marvel, 2/67); Rocky Mountain pedigree copy, CGC NM/MT 9.8, sold for $1,254 in 2012.

Original story page art from *Tales of Suspense* #84 featuring Captain America by Jack Kirby and Frank Giacoia; sold for $3,346 in 2009.

Captain America takes a tumble in *Tales of Suspense* #96 (Marvel, 12/67); CGC NM+ 9.6, sold for $262 in 2016.

▼ *Amazing Spider-Man King Size Annual #2 (Marvel, 1965); CGC NM+ 9.6, sold for $3,346 in 2016.*

▼ *Amazing Spider-Man King-Size Special #3 (Marvel, 1966); Pacific Coast pedigree copy, CGC NM+ 9.6, sold for $1,673 in 2016.*

▲ Amazing Spider-Man King-Size Special #4 (Marvel, 1967); Pacific Coast pedigree copy, CGC NM/MT 9.8, sold for $8,365 in 2016.

◄ Avengers King-Size Special #1 (Marvel, 1967); Boston pedigree copy, CGC NM/MT 9.8, sold for $4,780 in 2016.

▼ *Fantastic Four King-Size Annual #3 (Marvel, 1965); CGC NM+ 9.6, sold for $1,434 in 2016.*

▲ *Daredevil King-Size Special #1 (Marvel, 9/67); Twin Cities pedigree copy, CGC NM/MT 9.8, sold for $1,314 in 2011.*

▶ *Journey Into Mystery King-Size Special #1 (Marvel, 1965); Pacific Coast pedigree copy, CGC NM+ 9.6, sold for $7,170 in 2016.*

▶ *Fantastic Four King-Size Special #4 (Marvel, 11/66); Twin Cities pedigree copy, CGC NM/MT 9.8, sold for $2,868 in 2012.*

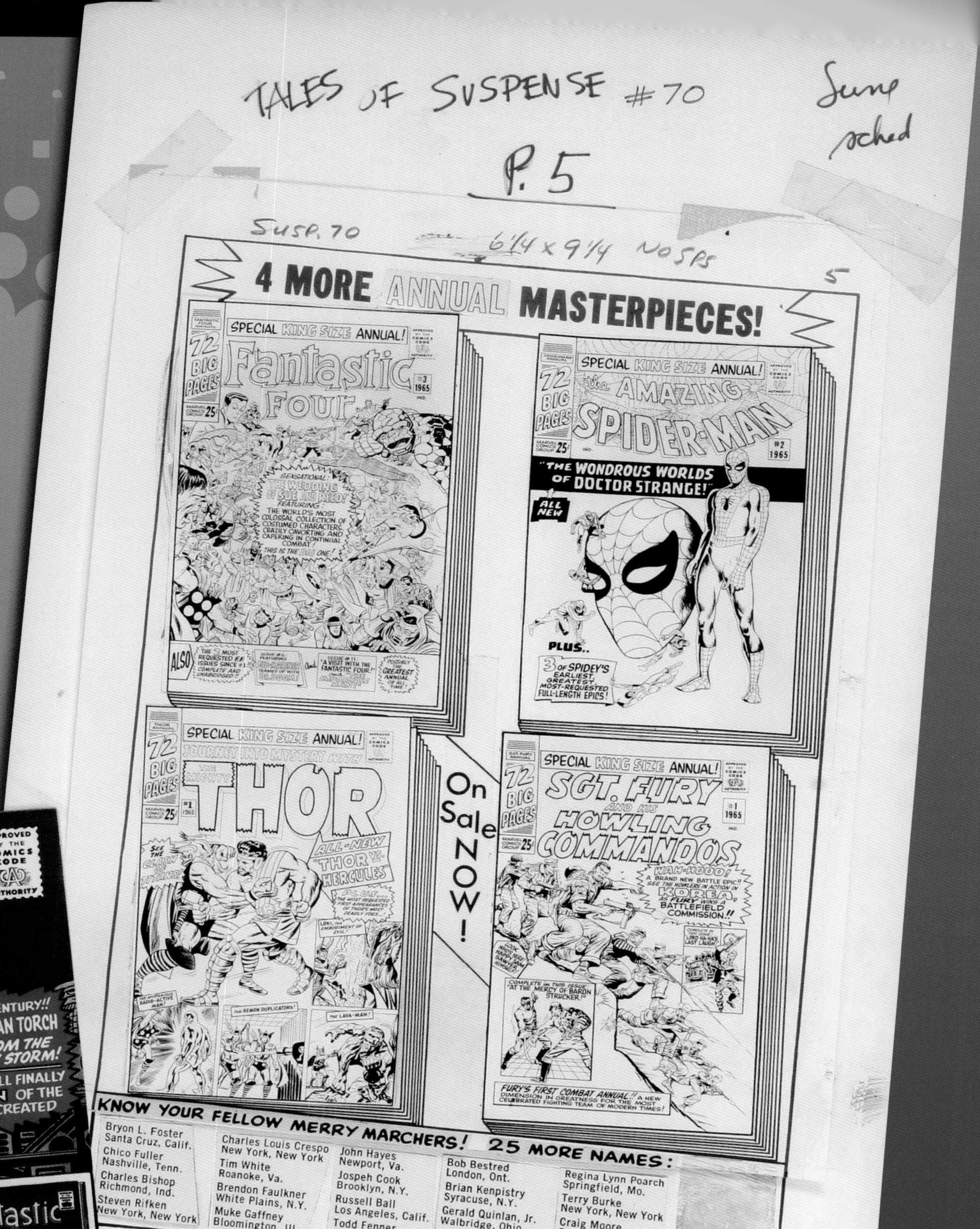

TALES OF SUSPENSE #70
June sched
P. 5
SUSP. 70
6 1/4 x 9 1/4 NO SPS
5
4 MORE ANNUAL MASTERPIECES!
SPECIAL KING SIZE ANNUAL!
72 BIG PAGES
Fantastic Four
#3 1965
SENSATIONAL: THE WEDDING OF SUE AND REED! FEATURING THE WORLD'S MOST COLOSSAL COLLECTION OF COSTUMED CHARACTERS CRAZILY CAVORTING AND CAPERING IN CONTINUAL COMBAT! THIS IS THE BIG ONE!
ALSO
"A VISIT WITH THE FANTASTIC FOUR!"
POSSIBLY THE GREATEST ANNUAL OF ALL TIME!
SPECIAL KING SIZE ANNUAL!
72 BIG PAGES
the AMAZING SPIDER-MAN
#2 1965
"THE WONDROUS WORLDS OF DOCTOR STRANGE!"
ALL NEW
PLUS..
3 OF SPIDEY'S EARLIEST, GREATEST, MOST-REQUESTED FULL-LENGTH EPICS!
SPECIAL KING SIZE ANNUAL!
72 BIG PAGES
JOURNEY INTO MYSTERY WITH THE MIGHTY THOR
#1 1965
ALL-NEW "THOR VS. HERCULES"
THE DEMON DUPLICATORS!
THE LAVA-MAN!
On Sale NOW!
SPECIAL KING SIZE ANNUAL!
72 BIG PAGES
SGT. FURY AND HIS HOWLING COMMANDOS
#1 1965
WAH-HOO! A BRAND NEW BATTLE EPIC! SEE THE HOWLERS IN ACTION IN KOREA, AS FURY WINS A BATTLEFIELD COMMISSION!!
COMPLETE IN THIS ISSUE! "AT THE MERCY OF BARON STRUCKER!"
FURY'S FIRST COMBAT ANNUAL!! A NEW DIMENSION IN GREATNESS FOR THE MOST CELEBRATED FIGHTING TEAM OF MODERN TIMES!
KNOW YOUR FELLOW MERRY MARCHERS! 25 MORE NAMES:
Bryon L. Foster Santa Cruz, Calif.
Chico Fuller Nashville, Tenn.
Charles Bishop Richmond, Ind.
Steven Rifken New York, New York
Charles Louis Crespo New York, New York
Tim White Roanoke, Va.
Brendon Faulkner White Plains, N.Y.
Muke Gaffney Bloomington, Ill.
John Hayes Newport, Va.
Jospeh Cook Brooklyn, N.Y.
Russell Ball Los Angeles, Calif.
Todd Fenner Chicago, Ill.
Bob Bestred London, Ont.
Brian Kenpistry Syracuse, N.Y.
Gerald Quinlan, Jr. Walbridge, Ohio
Woodward C. Warrick Grosse Pt., Mich.
Regina Lynn Poarch Springfield, Mo.
Terry Burke New York, New York
Craig Moore Carmichael, Calif.
John Boonstra Haledon, N. J.
568

A Marvel Comics Annuals house ad, made up mostly of production stats; sold for $836 in 2014.

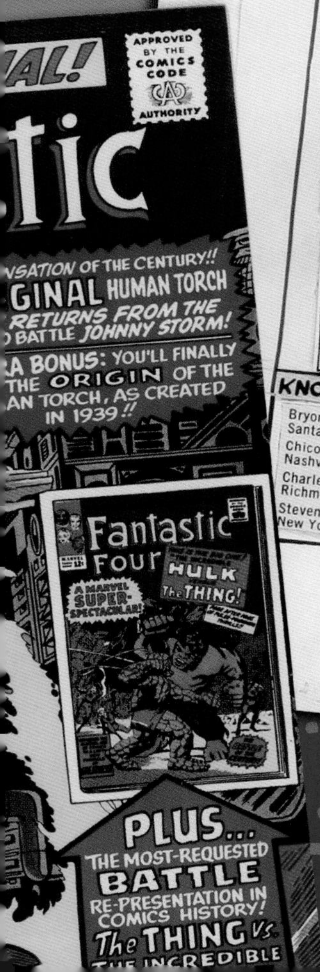

APPROVED BY THE COMICS CODE AUTHORITY
ORIGINAL HUMAN TORCH
RETURNS FROM THE
BATTLE JOHNNY STORM!
Fantastic Four
HULK
The THING!
PLUS...
THE MOST-REQUESTED BATTLE RE-PRESENTATION IN COMICS HISTORY!
The THING Vs.

Double-Dare Adventures #1, featuring B-Man (Harvey, 1966). First appearance and origin of Bee-Man, Magicmaster, and Glowing Gladiator. NM- 9.2, value in 2017 is $95.

CHAPTER 5

MEANWHILE, ACROSS TOWN: THE OTHER HEROES, 1965-67

AT THEIR peak of popularity in the mid-sixties, DC and Marvel found that the newsstand space for superhero comic books was beginning to get a little crowded. Some companies took their existing comic titles and added a hero or two.

American Comics Group (ACG) had been around since the 1940s and specialized in sci-fi and horror comics of a much tamer variety than the more lurid 1950s comics from EC and others. *Forbidden Worlds* began in 1951 with science fiction-themed stories, but with issue #125 (January-February 1965), Magicman was introduced. The front cover blurb said it all: "A new and thrilling hero — with all the strange powers of black magic! Meet … Magicman!" Following closely behind was Nemesis, first appearing in *Adventures into the Unknown* #154 (February 1965). Nemesis had a rather strange origin story. He was once government investigator Steve Flint, who gets himself run over by a train; his spirit is sent back to Earth as a cowl-wearing crime fighter, with strange ghostly powers. But ACG's strangest hero of all had to be the Fat Fury, a satirical version of the company's absurdly funny Herbie Popnecker, who first appeared back in 1958. Herbie jumped on the superhero bandwagon with *Herbie* #8 (March 1965), with the silliest hero costume ever — he wore a full-body suit of red underwear (with a drop seat in back), and a toilet plunger on his head like a helmet! I can't make this stuff up, folks!

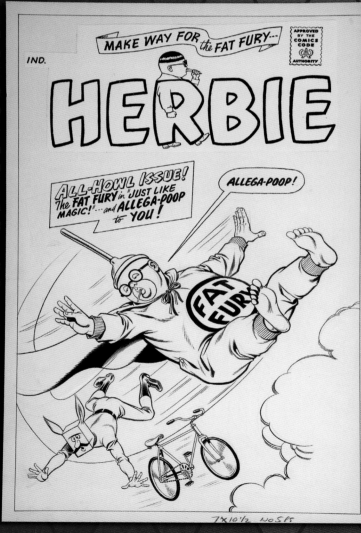

Original cover art to *Herbie* #22 by Kurt Shaffenberger (ACG, 1966); sold for $2,629 in 2009 (mis-identified as by Ogden Whitney, the regular *Herbie* story artist).

Original 1967 page 4 from *Captain Atom* #89 by Steve Ditko and Frank McLaughlin; sold for $1,135 in 2010.

Captain Atom #79 (Charlton, 2-3/66); Don and Maggie Thompson pedigree copy, CGC NM 9.4, sold for $125 in 2014.

▶ *Blue Beetle* #1 (Charlton, 6/67); CGC NM/MT 9.8, sold for $1,673 in 2014.

Mighty Crusaders #5 (Radio Comics, 6/66); Western Penn pedigree copy, CGC NM+ 9.6, sold for $95 in 2010.

Original ad page art featuring Steel Sterling by Paul Reinman; sold for $92 in 2005.

▶ Original concept art for *Spyman* by Jim Steranko, partially used as cover art for issue #1; sold for $3,585 in 2006.

ION. PERHAPS IT IS THE USE...
IT'S THE NOSE CONE PROTRUDING FROM THE ROOF...
ME SINCE ANYONE HAS VENTURED TO RING THE DOORBELL UND...

MIRACLES, INC.

I'M HUNGRY!

I'M DISAPPOINTED IN YOU MANLET! ALL YOU CAN THINK ABOUT IS YOUR BIRD SEED! MY DEFENSE SYSTEM IS NOW PERFECT! MISFIT, BRING ME THE ACTIVATOR!

DON'T BLOW YOUR COOL, PROF! IT'S LIKE, ON THE WAY!

DRESSED LIKE THIS?! I'LL HEAT UP LAST NIGHT'S POT!

HEY, THERMO! WHY DON'T YOU RUN DOWN TO THE STORE AND PICK UP SOME COFFEE?

THANKS FOR THE ICE CUBE SERVICE...

Original page 1 art from *Unearthly Spectaculars* #2 by Wally Wood; sold for $3,824 in 2015.

Atom was spotty, coming and going until 1967, when Ditko left Marvel and returned to Charlton. There, he spearheaded the company's Action Hero line, which also featured Ditko's The Question, The Peacemaker, Judomaster, Peter Cannon … Thunderbolt, and a revised Blue Beetle.

Over at Harvey Comics, almost everything except their humor line had been dropped, but the Superhero Revival and pop Art/Camp craze resulted in Harvey's Thriller line. In titles like *Double-Dare Adventures* and *Unearthly Spectaculars*, some of the wildest, most off-the-wall superheroes ever seen were introduced: Bee-Man (A NASA technician gets stung by Martian bees that had tagged along on the space probe, giving him super-strength and the ability to heal any wound quickly – perhaps the best of the Thriller heroes); Glowing Gladiator; Jack Q. Frost; Jigsaw (owned by Captain America co-creator Joe Simon, Jigsaw was the "man of a Thousand Parts," able to send his fist flying off his arm to punch a bad guy [or any other part – think about it a minute], and then reassemble at will); Pirana (another Joe Simon property, along with Spyman and Tiger Boy); plus a few more wild back-ups. None of these titles would last more than two or three issues.

Perhaps the most ambitious and successful, non-DC or Marvel superhero comics of the Silver Age were the ones published by Tower. The company was founded in 1965 as a division of Tower Books (paperback publishers), and lasted throughout the remaining Silver Age, finally ending in 1969. Tower had the supreme good fortune of enlisting Wally Wood (1927-1981), who had come into prominence at EC in the 1950s. Wood could handle just about any type of comic story, but he excelled in his sci-fi stories for EC's *Weird Science* and *Weird Fantasy*. Tower publisher/editor Harry Shorten gave Wood freedom to do his thing, and the result was *T.H.U.N.D.E.R. Agents*. This was a strange but highly popular feature that combined superhero and spy concepts into a team consisting of Dynamo, NoMan, and Menthor, plus a few later

Archie Comics got into the act by resurrecting a few of the old MLJ heroes like the Shield, the Comet, and the Black Hood. They were teamed with heroes created a few years earlier (The Fly, aka Fly-Man and The Jaguar) to form *The Mighty Crusaders*. This heroic team never really caught on, lasting only seven issues. There would be periodic rivals in years to come.

Charlton Comics had existed for years as a low-budget line notorious for their low pay to creators, and cheap-looking comics printed on coarse newsprint. They had inherited the Blue Beetle, a Golden Age hero once popular enough to rate his own daily comic strip. But the best the company had to offer was Captain Atom, who first appeared in *Space Adventures* #33 (March 1960). Artist Steve Ditko created Captain Atom with writer Joe Gill, and he proved popular enough to last beyond the life of the company; when Charlton gave it all up in 1984, DC acquired him, along with a few other properties. However, the publication history for Captain

Original splash page art from *Dynamo* #2 by George Tuska; entire ten-page story art sold for $2,031 in 2016.

arrivals like The Raven and a group of non-powered agents, the T.H.U.N.D.E.R. Squad. By the way, those initials stand for The Higher United Nations Defense Enforcement Reserves. Wonder how long it took to figure that one out?

Here's a brief rundown of the three main T.H.U.N.D.E.R. Agents:

Dynamo: Spy agent Leonard Brown receives the Thunder Belt, which changes his body's mass and atomic structure, increasing his strength by 100 percent, but he can only wear the belt for 30 minutes at a time, as it causes an enormous energy drain. Brown uses the belt to fight international crime as Dynamo. With the belt, he can leap hundreds of feet into the air, and survive bullets or other projectiles short of armor-piercing shells.

NoMan: 76-year-old wheelchair-bound scientist Dr. Anthony Dunn, who is near death, agrees to an experiment that transfers his consciousness to a specially-designed android body. This body weighs 350 pounds and possesses superhuman strength. There are multiple android bodies (built at a cost

A 1978 photo by Gil Ortiz of Wally Wood with the *Dynamo* #3 cover art displayed on the wall of his Darby, Connecticut, studio.

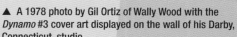

◄ Original cover art for *Dynamo* #3 by Wally Wood and Dan Adkins; sold for $21,850 in 2004.

Super Goof #1 (Gold Key, 10/65); CGC NM 9.4, sold for $262 in 2007.

► *Magnus, Robot Fighter* #14 (Gold Key, 5/66); CGC NM/MT 9.8, sold for $693 in 2014.

of $1,000,000 each), which Dr. Dunn can now assume at will, whenever necessary. He is also equipped with a cloak of invisibility, activated by the cloak's fastener dial. There is a radio receiver built into the temple of each android body, which is connected to the T.H.U.N.D.E.R. Agents headquarters. Dr. Dunn must transfer his consciousness to another android body before the one he is inhabiting is destroyed, or he will die.

Menthor: Double-agent Janus was a T.H.U.N.D.E.R. recruit, but was actually working for Warlord (the main threat to the agency) when he agrees to try out a special helmet; it gives him the power to read minds, perform computer-fast calculations, and feed on the strength of others, and he can manipulate solid objects with his mental energy. The helmet has a hidden power, though: it works on the subconscious, forcing the wearer to do good. When Janus is killed by a Warlord ally, the helmet is passed on to the other T.H.U.N.D.E.R. Agents.

In addition to Wally Wood, there are several notable artists who drew the Tower Comics stories, including Reed Crandall (another EC staffer), Gil Kane, Steve Ditko, Roger Brand, Steve Skeates, Richard Bassford, and Dan Adkins. Writers included Len Brown, Bill Pearson, and Russ Jones (who was also an artist).

Tower also published a sister title, *U.N.D.E.R.S.E.A. Agent*, as a six-issue series. The T.H.U.N.D.E.R. Agents live on today, having been picked up by DC in 2010.

While mainly known for their licensed properties like Donald Duck, Little Lulu, and Bugs Bunny, Gold Key had a few original series titles that veered close to superhero territory. Some featured pretty much out-and-out superheroes, like *Doctor Solar, Man of the Atom*, and *Magnus, Robot Fighter*; others were more adventure-driven characters with jungle or science fiction themes: *M.A.R.S. Patrol Total War, Mighty Samson, Tragg and the Sky Gods*, and *Tiger Girl*. A few licensed properties had superhero-styled characters, like *Flash Gordon, The Green Hornet* (a TV tie-in based on a Golden Age comic character and radio star), *The Phantom*, and *Supercar*. One Disney

character actually became a humorous superhero in 1965: none other than Goofy as *Super Goof*. Gold Key had originally been known as Dell Comics, but in the early sixties, they split into two separate companies. Dell continued on, with a few unique superhero titles of its own (some only lasting an issue or two), like *Neutro, Nukla, Frankenstein* (a bizarre attempt to mix a classic horror character with superheroes; there were also "new" versions of Werewolf and Dracula). Many were closer to adventure than superhero-based: *Kona, Monarch of Monster Isle, Tonka the Jungle King*, and *Turok, Son of Stone*.

There's one more hero that must be mentioned here, but first, a little history of the creators. Artist C. C. Beck and writer Otto Binder originated what was, at one time, the most popular and best-selling superhero comic of the Golden Age: Fawcett's Captain Marvel. The "Big Red Cheese" had a unique style that was more playful than most costumed superheroes, and was loved by young and old alike (Radar O'Reilly on the classic TV sitcom, *M.A.S.H.*, often spoke of his love for Captain Marvel comic books, as did Gomer on *The Andy Griffith Show*, with his slang use of the "magic word," Shazam).

There was a lawsuit between Fawcett and DC, who claimed the good Captain was a rip-off of Superman, and the case finally ended in the mid-fifties with Fawcett dropping the character's line of titles.

Jump to 1966, when small independent publisher Lightning Comics published the first issue of *Fatman the Human Flying Saucer* by Beck and Binder. The series was touted as "Written and drawn by the creators of the original Captain Marvel," and the look and feel of each of the three 64-page issues was much like that beloved Golden Age series – whimsical and fun, with the main character dressed in a similar costume to that earlier hero, only in green instead of red. There were numerous references to Captain Marvel, including Fatman's sidekick, who looked like a skinny version of Cap's alter-ego, Billy Batson, who even liked to exclaim "Holey Moley," just as Billy did.

It was all too short-lived, ending with the third issue, but the series paved the way for a strong nostalgia movement for 1940s comics that peaked in the 1970s. Seek this one out!

▶ Original cover art for *Fatman* #3 by C. C. Beck; sold for $1,063 in 2002.

From left: *Fatman* #1 (Lightning Comics, 10/67); Boston pedigree copy, CGC NM 9.4, sold for $95 in 2015. *Fatman* #2 (Lightning Comics, 6/67); CGC NM+ 9.6, sold for $131 in 2012.

Mighty Comics #50 (Radio Comics, 10/67); CGC NM- 9.2, sold for $38 in 2012.

The Mighty Crusaders #6 (Radio Comics, 8/66); Rocky Mountain pedigree copy, CGC NM+ 9.6, sold for $191 in 2016.

▶ Original story page art from *The Mighty Crusaders* #1 by Paul Reinman; sold for $382 in 2016.

Original story page art from *Fly Man* #31 by Paul Reinman; sold for $382 in 2016.

▶ *Fly Man* #35 (Archie, 1/66); Boston pedigree copy, CGC NM/MT 9.8, sold for $262 in 2015.

◀ *The Shadow* #5 (Archie, 3/65); Western Penn pedigree, CGC NM/ MT 9.8, sold for $131 in 2010.

▲ *Fly Man* #39 (Archie, 9/66); Boston pedigree copy, CGC NM+ 9.6, sold for $215 in 2015.

◀ *The Shadow* #6 (Archie, 5/65); Western Penn pedigree, CGC VF/NM 9.0, sold for $69 in 2010.

▶ Original cover art by Bob White for *Life With Archie* #42 (Archie, 1965); first appearance of Captain Pureheart. Sold for $2,270 in 2013.

▲ Three Archie character superhero comic books; Average VF condition, sold as part of a group of four books for $84 in 2011.

▶ *The Peacemaker* #1 (Charlton, 3/67); CGC NM-9.2, sold for $69 in 2015.

CAPTAIN ATOM AND CHARLTON HEROES

Captain Atom #83 (Charlton, 11/66); CGC NM 9.4, sold for $1,912 in 2016.

Captain Atom #87 (Charlton, 8/67); Don and Maggie Thompson pedigree copy, CGC NM 9.4, sold for $239 in 2014.

◄ Judo Master #98 (Charlton, 12/67); Western Penn pedigree copy, CGC NM+ 9.6, sold for $79 in 2010.

Original unpublished cover art intended for *Captain Atom* #89 by Steve Ditko; sold for $7,767 in 2014.

◄ *Doctor Solar, Man of the Atom* #17 (Gold Key, 9/66); File Copy, CGC NM+ 9.6, sold for $239 in 2016.

▼ *Frankenstein* #3 (Dell, 12/66); CGC NM+ 9.6, sold for $119 in 2015.

► *Nukla* #1 (Dell, 10-12/65); File Copy, CGC NM+ 9.6, sold for $86 in 2010.

◄ *The Green Hornet* #1 (Gold Key, 2/67); Boston pedigree copy, CGC NM 9.4, sold for $717 in 2015.

Spyman #2 (Harvey, 12/66); White Mountain pedigree copy, CGC NM- 9.2, sold for $92 in 2016.

Double-Dare Adventures #2, featuring B-Man (Harvey, 1966); NM- 92, value in 2017 is $65.

◄ Jigsaw #2 (Harvey, 12/66); CGC NM+ 9.6, sold for $86 in 2014.

► Fighting American #1 (Harvey, 10/66); Twin Cities pedigree copy, CGC NM/MT 9.8, sold for $358 in 2013.

TOWER COMICS: DYNAMO & NOMAN

Dynamo #3 (Tower, 3/67); CGC NM+ 9.6, sold for $262 in 2015.

Dynamo #1 (Tower, 8/66); CBCS NM 9.4, sold for $107 in 2015.

NoMan #1 (Tower, 11/66); CGC NM+ 9.6, sold for $418 in 2015.

NoMan #2 (Tower, 3/67); CGC NM- 9.2, sold for $84 in 2016.

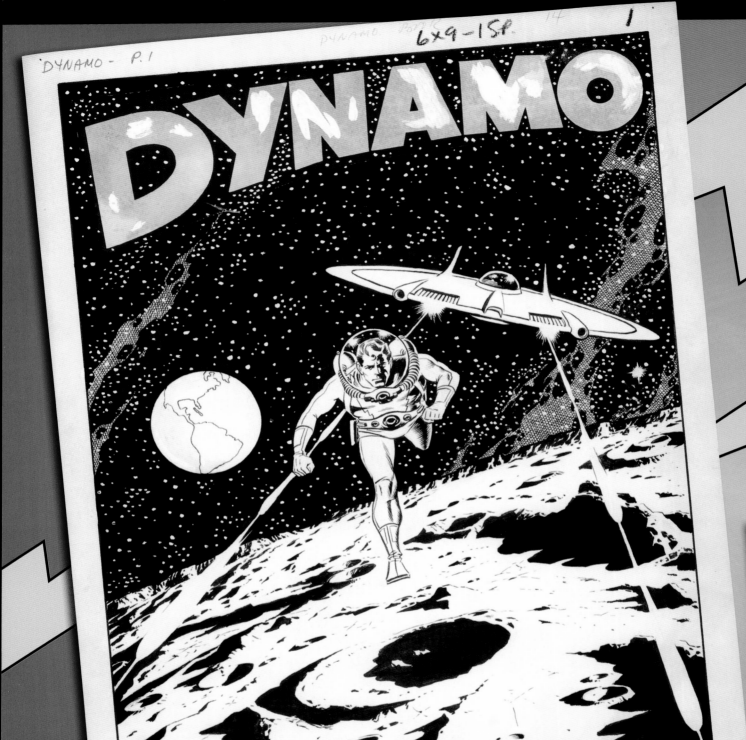

Original splash page art from *Dynamo* #1 by Wally Wood and Dan Adkins; sold for $21,510 in 2012.

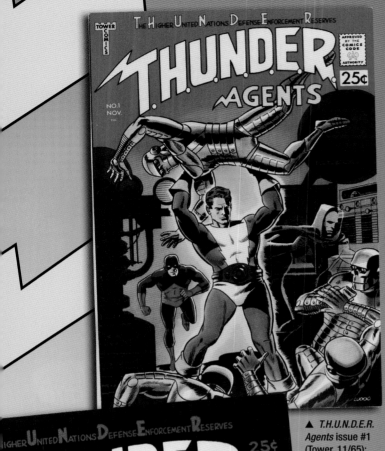

▲ *T.H.U.N.D.E.R. Agents* issue #1 (Tower, 11/65); Twin Cities pedigree copy, CGC NM+ 9.6, sold for $776 in 2012.

▲ *T.H.U.N.D.E.R. Agents* issue #2 (Tower, 1/66); Boston pedigree copy, CGC NM/MT 9.8, sold for $478 in 2015.

T.H.U.N.D.E.R. Agents issue #5 (Tower, 6/66); CGC NM+ 9.6, sold for $286 in 2015.

▲ *T.H.U.N.D.E.R. Agents* issue #6 (Tower, 7/66); CGC NM+ 9.6, sold for $382 in 2016.

HERBIE AND ACG HEROES,
1965–1967

◄ *Herbie* #16 (ACG, 3/66); Twin Cities pedigree copy, CGC NM/MT 9.8, sold for $388 in 2011.

▼ *Adventures Into the Unknown* #162 (ACG, 2/66) featuring Nemesis; CGC NM 9.4, sold for $63 in 2009.

◄ *Forbidden Worlds* #130 (ACG, 9/65) featuring Magicman; CGC VF 8.0, sold for $28 in 2013.

Herbie #10 (ACG, 6-7/65); Twin Cities pedigree copy, CGC NM- 9.2, sold for $89 in 2012.

Herbie #8 (ACG, 3/65) Qualified grade: cover detached from top staple. Twin Cities pedigree copy, CGC Qualified NM+ 9.6, sold for $131 in 2011.

Original cover art for *Action Comics* #361 by Neal Adams; sold for $10,465 in 2010.

CHAPTER 6

DAWN OF A NEW ERA
1968-69

THE BRIGHT, SPLASHY, "Zap! Pow!" pop era in comics was pretty short-lived. Despite changes in the *Batman* TV series involving adding Batgirl (played nicely by the oh-so-lovely Yvonne Craig) and changing the format to once-a-week, self-contained episodes, the ratings had dropped significantly by the third season (1967-68). The superhero craze died down, leaving it back with the "fanboys" who were regular comic buyers. The *Batman* comic book stories had briefly taken their cue from the show, but now they began to reflect a much darker, more serious tone. Batman had begun in 1939 as a dark, moody series, and now that was coming back full circle. The change was not overnight — stories still had titles like "The Riddler's Prison-Puzzle Problem!" (*Detective Comics* #377, July 1968) and "The Fortune-Cookie Caper!" (*Detective Comics* #383, January 1969), but the cover color schemes were definitely getting darker. By *Detective Comics* #386 (April 1969), the images were shadow-heavy and grim.

About this time, artist Neal Adams began a series of stories featuring the Caped Crusader that would turn the world of comics fandom upside-down. Adams was a skilled illustrator who employed dramatic "camera" angles in his comics work. In 1962, he had been hired to draw the daily *Ben Casey* newspaper comic strip, a straight-forward adaptation of the popular dramatic TV series starring Vince Edwards;

although stylized, his artwork gave the daily (and later Sunday) strips a photo-realist look. Adams also worked in advertising during this time. In 1967, he began doing work for DC, doing war and humor stories, but also covers for *Action Comics* and *Superman's Girl Friend, Lois Lane*. Batman was his preference, though, and when he finally got a chance to draw the character (on the cover of *The Brave and the Bold* #75; November

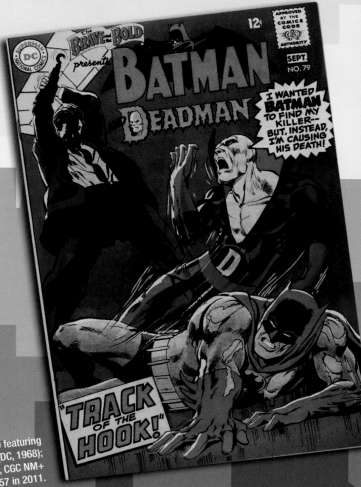

Brave and the Bold #79 featuring Batman and The Spectre (DC, 1968); Savannah pedigree copy, CGC NM+ 9.6, sold for $657 in 2011.

Strange Adventures #205 (DC, 10/67), first appearance of Deadman; CGC NM 9.4, sold for $2,987 in 2011.

The Spectre #2 (DC, 1-2/68); Pacific Coast pedigree, CGC NM/MT 9.8, sold for $836 in 2013.

1967), DC editors were impressed (Adams had been turned down for Batman several times before). Finally, with *World's Finest* #175 (May 1968), he got the chance to do a complete story featuring the Gotham Guardian.

But before Batman, Neal Adams had made his distinctive mark on one of DC's darkest comic characters ever. Deadman had first appeared in *Strange Adventures* #205, drawn by Carmine Infantino. With the next issue, Adams (with inker George Roussos) handled both the cover and interior art chores, with spectacular results. Deadman was "really" a dead man, a circus trapeze artist named Boston Brand, who uses "Deadman" as a stage name. Brand gets assassinated by an underworld killer, and through intervention of "Hindu god" Rama Kushna, he returns to life to avenge his own death.

Another other-worldly character Neal Adams worked on in the late sixties was The Spectre. Similar to Deadman, The Spectre had been killed by villains; his spirit returned to

Earth as a sort of ghostly avenger. This was a Golden Age hero who debuted in *More Fun Comics* #51 (January 1940). The character was brought back in *Showcase* #60 (February 1966). Adams drew the Spectre on a regular basis, beginning with issue #2 of the character's own title (January-February 1968), taking over from artist Murphy Anderson.

These were both dark characters, atypical of superheroes like Superman and the Flash. The stories attracted older readers, which was the ultimate goal — to get comic books out of the "disposable entertainment for children" gutter.

SUPERMAN GETS GRITTIER

Superman, too, was undergoing some changes. The stories were getting grittier and tougher, although the story art provided by Curt Swan still looked pretty close to what had come before. The covers, though, were definitely more dramatic, especially when drawn by Neal Adams. He would handle cover chores for the Man of

Superman #213 (DC, 1/69); Pacific Coast pedigree copy, CGC NM/MT 9.8, sold for $2,031 in 2011.

Beware the Creeper #5 (DC, 2/69); CBCS NM/MT 9.8, sold for $239 in 2016.

Brother Power the Geek #1 (DC, 10/68); Northland pedigree copy, CGC NM 9.4, sold for $203 in 2016.

Steel beginning with *Superman* #204, with the art team of Ross Andru and Mike Esposito replacing Swan on the inside pages. Swan would soon return, but it was obvious the world had changed for Clark Kent and his friends. In "The Orphans of Space" (*Superman* #213, January 1969), Superman actually blows up the world, leaving only him, Supergirl, and pet dog Krypto as survivors. It turned out to be a Red Kryptonite hallucination. Within a short span of time, even Kryptonite would change, and these "red herring" stories would be a thing of the past.

ODDBALL SUPERHEROES

DC introduced some odd superheroes in the late 1960s. Take, for instance, The Creeper. Steve Ditko (yes, him again) created him as someone with super strength and stamina (pretty essential elements for any comic book hero), but also with the ability to cause physical pain to his opponents by laughing at them. This strange-looking character, with his green hair, yellow tights, and

Metamorpho #16 (DC, 1-2/68); Twin Cities pedigree copy, CGC NM+ 9.6, sold for $717 in 2011.

Metal Men #30 (DC, 2-3/68); CGC NM+ 9.6, sold for $191 in 2012.

a red cape that looked more like flowing hair than cloth, first saw print in *Showcase* #73 (March 1968), followed by a series that ran a scant six issues. However, he would resurface several times in later years.

Stranger still was *Brother Power the Geek*. Created by Joe Simon (another familiar name), this series blended superheroes with Frankenstein — Brother Power was an abandoned mannequin who came to life when struck by lightning, which not only animated him, but also gave him super strength and speed. An odd character, involved with then-trendy hippie sub-culture. It was not well liked by readers, and even less so by the DC editorial staff. The series was cancelled after the second issue.

Of course, there were odd super-powered characters throughout DC's Silver Age output, like *Metamorpho, the Element Man*, who could change any part of his body into any element found in the human body, after exposure to a radioactive meteorite. Premiering in *Brave and the Bold* #57 (January 1965), he was all over the DC Universe. His 17-issue series ended in 1968. *The Metal Men* was a similar group in that each member was composed of a different metal (oh yeah, they were also humanized robots); their series ran from 1963 to 1970.

The Phantom Stranger had appeared in a short-lived early 1950s series; he returned to the fold in *Showcase* #80 (February 1969). He wasn't quite a superhero, but more like a supernatural detective. Nightmaster (*Showcase* #82, May 1969) had the tights and cape of a typical superhero, but was actually a "sword and sorcery" character with a touch of the supernatural.

MARVEL TAKES SOME MISSTEPS

Marvel went through a rough patch in 1968. The company was sold to Martin S. Ackerman, who immediately upped the number of publications. Quality began to drop, as did sales, which had been steadily climbing each preceding year. The expansion gave Captain America, Iron Man, Thor, Doctor Strange, and Sub-Mariner their own titles, after appearing as features in *Tales of Suspense, Strange Tales, Journey Into Mystery*, and *Tales to Astonish*.

Marvel's main powerhouse artist, Jack Kirby,

Iron Man #1 (Marvel, 5/68), CGC NM/MT 9.8, sold for $15,535 in 2016.

In time, an exodus of talent left the company, and those who stayed were apparently treated badly by the new owners. However, there were a few bright spots during this somewhat shaky time. Jim Steranko and Neal Adams both did exceptional work for the company, and newcomer Barry Smith (or, Windsor-Smith, as he is now credited) showed real potential. All three men worked on faltering title *X-Men* during this time, turning out fantastic graphic designs for stories written by Roy Thomas. Smith handled art chores a few issues of *The Avengers* as well.

Overall, though, there was a noticeable drop in quality that would take several years to move past. The House of Ideas had sold out to corporate bean counters, who cared only about the bottom line. Sadly, this loss of interest in content by management was directly opposite to what made Marvel great in the first place.

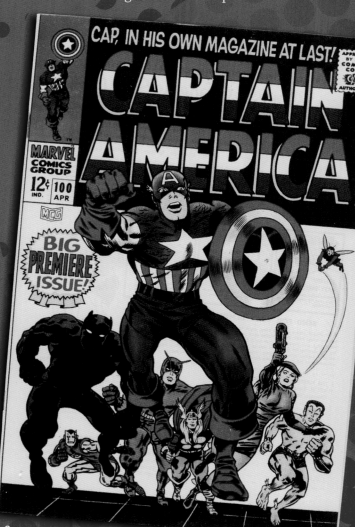

Captain America #100 (Marvel, 3/68); CGC NM/MT 9.8 sold for $5,258 in 2016.

started to simplify his page layouts with fewer panels, supposedly after being turned down for a raise by Stan Lee. Other artists followed suit, and soon the page size for original artwork was reduced, meaning less detail on each page. Stories became more stretched out, meaning kids had to buy more comic books to read a single story; sharp-eyed readers noticed the trend, and complained in letter columns. Also, Marvel stepped back from tackling big issues as in years before. The year 1968 was tumultuous, with assassinations, protests over the war in Vietnam, and a contentious presidential election that brought right-winger Richard Nixon to the White House. A fear of controversy meant Marvel was no longer the "cutting edge" comic publisher fans had come to know and love. And with so many titles being pumped out each month, it became impossible for Stan Lee to be fully involved in every storyline.

iN MY NEiGHBORHOOD

LIKE MOST BOYS MY age in the sixties, I began to "grow out" of comic book collecting, and by 1968, I had pretty much stopped buying comics altogether, spending my allowance instead on monster magazines like *Famous*

Monsters of Filmland, *Modern Monsters*, and *Castle of Frankenstein*. I also got into model car kits around this time.

I was a bit slow to really catch on to the rock 'n' roll revolution taking place in the sixties, but by 1968, buying records was a huge deal with me. I went for 45 RPM singles first, as they were affordable, but early in 1968, I discovered "cut-out" bins stuffed with record albums at my local Kmart; my first purchases were *Daydream* by the Lovin' Spoonful, and *Once Upon a Dream* by The Rascals. These were mono records that were being phased out in favor of stereo, but since I had only a small, old record player given to me on my third birthday that played only in mono, I didn't care.

But by the end of 1969, I got that big book of old *Buck Rogers* newspaper strips, and the urge to read comics slowly creeped back into by consciousness.

POP CULTURE EVENTS, 1968-69

JANUARY 1968 . . Rowan & Martin's *Laugh-In* premieres on NBC-TV; the Tet Offensive begins in Vietnam

APRIL 1968 . . . . Stanley Kubrick's landmark film, *2001: A Space Odyssey*, opens; *Planet of the Apes* movie is released; Martin Luther King Jr. is assassinated, resulting in riots across the US; the Civil Rights Act is signed into law

MAY 1968 . . . . . . The Beatles create Apple Records

JUNE 1968 . . . . . . Pop Artist Andy Warhol is shot and wounded by Valerie Solanas; presidential candidate Senator Robert Kennedy is shot and killed; movie *Rosemary's Baby* is released

AUGUST 1968 . . . . Protests and riots occur at the Democratic National Convention in Chicago

SEPTEMBER 1968 . *Hawaii Five-O* and *60 Minutes* debut on CBS-TV

OCTOBER 1968 . . . Led Zeppelin play their first show, at Surrey University in the UK

NOVEMBER 1968 . . Richard Nixon is elected president

DECEMBER 1968 . . Apollo 8 astronauts make the first orbit around the moon

JANUARY 1969 . . . The Beatles play live for the last time, recording tracks on the roof of Apple Records; the first Led Zeppelin album is released

MARCH 1969 . . . . John Lennon marries Yoko Ono and they stage their Bed-In for Peace

MAY 1969 . . . . The first death from AIDS is reported

JULY 1969 . . . . . . Former member of The Rolling Stones, Brain Jones, dies; Apollo 11 astronauts Neil Armstrong and Buzz Aldrin are the first to land on the moon

AUGUST 1969 . . . . The followers of Charles Manson begin their killing spree; the Woodstock Festival is held in upstate New York

SEPTEMBER 1969 . *Scooby-Doo, Where Are You?* animated series premieres on CBS-TV; last Warner Brothers Merrie Melodies cartoon, *Injun Trouble*, is released to theaters; *The Brady Bunch* premieres on ABC-TV; *Abbey Road* is released by The Beatles

OCTOBER 1969 . . . *Monty Python's Flying Circus* debuts on UK television; the New York Mets win the World Series

NOVEMBER 1969 . . Pioneering children's TV program, *Sesame Street*, premieres; second US moon flight occurs

DECEMBER 1969 . . The tragic, violent Altamont Free Concert, headlined by The Rolling Stones, occurs, considered by many as "the end of the sixties"

Superboy #160 (DC, 10/68); Twin Cities pedigree copy, CGC NM/MT 9.8, sold for $1,015 in 2011.

▲ Action Comics #359 (DC, 2/68); Twin Cities pedigree copy, CGC NM/MT 9.8, sold for $1,912 in 2011.

◄ The Spectre #4 (DC, 6/68); Twin Cities pedigree copy, CGC NM/MT 9.8, sold for $717 in 2011.

► Adventure Comics #371 (DC, 8/68); CGC NM+ 9.6, sold for $501 in 2015.

Batman #203 aka *80 Page Giant #49* (DC, 8/68); Newsstand Mint Collection pedigree copy, CBCS NM-9.2, sold for $185 in 2016.

Batman #217 (DC, 12/69); CGC NM 9.4, sold for $478 in 2016.

Detective Comics #372 (DC, 2/68); CGC NM 9.4, sold for $143 in 2015.

Original cover art for *Justice League of America* #66 by Neal Adams; sold for $41,825 in 2016.

Superman's Pal Jimmy Olsen #111 (DC, 6/68); Twin Cities pedigree copy, CGC NM/MT 9.8, sold for $239 in 2012.

Green Lantern #63 (DC, 9/68); Twin Cities pedigree copy, CGC NM+ 9.6, sold for $388 in 2011.

Detective Comics #388 Joker Cover (DC, 6/69); Savannah pedigree copy, CGC NM+ 9.6, sold for $1,673 in 2011.

Justice League of America #61 (DC, 3/68); CBCS NM/MT 9.8, sold for $1,135 in 2016.

BIG-SCREEN SUPERHEROES

WONDER WOMAN'S LASTING LEGACY

The cultural impact of Wonder Woman has been felt since she made her comic-book debut in 1941, and never more so than today. She is one of the most well-known superheroes, but it still took the character 75 years to reach the milestone of appearing in the first female hero standalone feature film: 2017's aptly titled *Wonder Woman*.

Starring Gal Gadot, the movie has been a bona fide box office blockbuster, earning more than $412.5 million domestically and $821.7 million globally as of December 2017 and becoming Warner Bros.' third-highest grossing film of all time. Director Patty Jenkins is also the first woman to helm a big-budget superhero movie.

But decades before Gadot debuted as Wonder Woman in the DC film universe to near universal praise, the general public was most familiar with the Amazon superhero from the 1970s' TV series starring Lynda Carter, who became a pop-culture icon, and whose portrayal of the character became the definitive Wonder Woman for many for over 40 years.

Carter brought Diana Prince/Wonder Woman to life on the small screen for the mainstream, from 1975 to 1979, first on ABC, and then on CBS for seasons 2 and 3. The show itself has a skillful camp style, with Wonder Woman catching baddies in her magic lasso, deflecting bullets with her bracelets, flying in her invisible airplane, and doing a classic ballerina spin to change identities. Whereas the show could be campy and cheesy, Carter was sincere in her performance and her character was powerful, kind, and a force to be reckoned with. Carter left such a potent impression with her iconic portrayal that DC developed a comic book series, Wonder Woman 77, set in the TV series continuity.

With Carter's portrayal being such a strong and consistent presence within pop culture after all these years, it's no surprise that Jenkins has praised the legacy of Carter, and credits her for helping pave the way for the film and its success.

DC Films/Warner Bros. Pictures

Bruce Lansbury Productions, Ltd./ Warner Bros. Television/DC Comics/ABC

Lynda Carter as Wonder Woman, left, and Gal Gadot as the character, top.

Wonder Woman #178 (DC, 9-10/68); Twin Cities pedigree, CGC NM+ 9.6, sold for $1,314 in 2011.

X-Men #58 (Marvel, 7/69); Pacific Coast pedigree copy, CGC NM/MT 9.8, sold for $3,226 in 2012.

X-Men #57 (Marvel, 6/69); CGC NM/MT 9.8, sold for $4,182 in 2012.

X-Men #56 (Marvel, 5/69); CGC VF/NM 9.0, sold for $131 in 2013.

Original story page art from *X-Men* #60 by Neal Adams and Tom Palmer; sold for $4,780 in 2012.

◄ Original cover art to *The Amazing Spider-Man* #62 by John Romita Sr.; sold for $179,250 in 2016.

► *Amazing Spider-Man* #66 (Marvel, 11/68); CGC NM+ 9.6, sold for $365 in 2017.

◄ *Amazing Spider-Man* #68 (Marvel, 1/69); CGC NM/MT 9.8, sold for $2,270 in 2012.

► *Amazing Spider-Man* #72 (Marvel, 5/69); Twin Cities pedigree copy, CGC NM/MT, sold for $4,481 in 2011.

SUPERMAN FAMILY, 1968–69

▼ *Action Comics #373 aka Giant G57, Supergirl issue (DC, 3/69); CGC NM+ 9.6, sold for $286 in 2015.*

▼ *Superboy #144 (DC, 1/68); CGC NM 9.4, sold for $89 in 2016.*

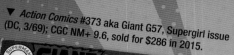

▼ *Superman #209 (DC, 8/68); Pacific Coast pedigree copy, CGC NM/MT 9.8, sold for $2,031 in 2011.*

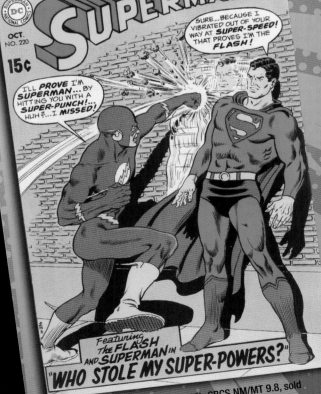

▲ *Superman #220 (DC, 10/69); CBCS NM/MT 9.8, sold for $298 in 2016.*

Original cover art to
Thor #157 by Jack
Kirby and Vince
Colletta; sold for
$63,335 in 2016.

Thor #154 (Marvel,
7/68); CGC NM/MT
9.8, sold for $507
in 2012.

Captain America #109
(Marvel, 1/69); front
cover signed by Stan
Lee, CGC NM/MT 9.8,
sold for $1,792 in 2016.

MORE MARVEL HEROES, 1968-69

▼ *Sub-Mariner* #1 (Marvel, 5/68); CGC NM/MT 9.8, sold for $2,390 in 2014.

▲ Original cover art to *Strange Tales* #164 featuring Doctor Strange, by Dan Adkins; sold for $71,700 in 2016.

▶ *Tales to Astonish* #100 Sub-Mariner and Hulk cover (Marvel, 2/68); CGC NM/MT 9.8, sold for $1.314 in 2016.

◀ *Iron Man and Sub-Mariner* #1 (only issue, Marvel, 4/68); CGC NM/MT 9.8, sold for $6,273 in 2016.

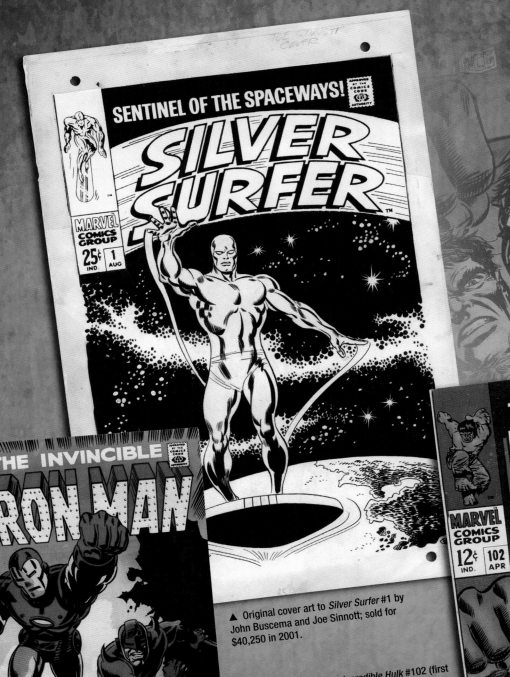

▲ Original cover art to *Silver Surfer* #1 by John Buscema and Joe Sinnott; sold for $40,250 in 2001.

▶ *Incredible Hulk* #102 (first issue of new series, Marvel, 4/68); CGC NM/MT 9.8, sold for $4,302 in 2016.

◀ *Iron Man* #16 (Marvel, 8/69); Twin Cities pedigree copy, CGC NM/MT 9.8, sold for $746 in 2011.

▲ X-Men #50 (Marvel, 11/68); CGC NM/MT 9.8, sold for $1,792 in 2015.

Incredible Hulk Annual (King Size Special) #1 (Marvel, 10/68); Pacific Coast pedigree copy, CGC NM+ 9.6, sold for $1,165 in 2016.

◀ Captain America #111 (Marvel, 3/69); CGC NM+ 9.6, sold for $358 in 2015.

Original cover art to *Green Lantern #76* by Neal Adams; sold for $442,150 in 2015.

CHAPTER 7

THINGS TO COME

JUST AROUND the corner from the 1960s, the next great era in American comic books – the Bronze Age – would begin with issue #76 of *Green Lantern*. Cover-dated April 1970, this was a high water mark for DC, which found itself suddenly hip and relevant after years of playing it relatively safe. It had seemed that Marvel and DC had somehow traded places, as that once-hip publisher had grown stale and fearful of controversy.

These new Green Lantern tales paired him with the Green Arrow; the stories were written by Denny O'Neil, with mind-blowing art from Neal Adams. The cover to *Green Lantern #76* let us know right away that big changes were in store. Over the course of thirteen issues, this new Green Team traveled the country, along with the Green Arrow's girlfriend, the Black Canary. Ecology, the plight of Native Americans, poverty, political oppression – all were topics of the series. The most dramatic challenge to the heroes turned out to be drugs; Green Arrow's long-time youthful sidekick Speedy is revealed to be a teenaged heroin addict, in a gut-wrenching two-part story printed in issues #85 (August-September 1971) and #86 (October-November 1971). Drug use had always been a taboo subject, thanks to the Comics Code, but times were changing, and both issues were granted the Code seal on their covers.

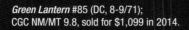

Green Lantern #85 (DC, 8-9/71); CGC NM/MT 9.8, sold for $1,099 in 2014.

Original story page 19 art from *Green Lantern* #85, with Green Lantern on a drug-induced "bad trip" by Neal Adams; sold for $10,157 in 2015.

Batman #237 (DC, 12/71); Don/Maggie Thompson pedigree copy, CGC NM+ 9.6, sold for $621 in 2014.

Superman #233 (DC, 1/71); CGC NM 9.4, sold for $549 in 2015.

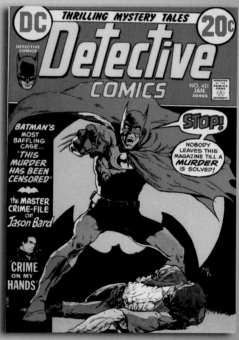

Detective Comics #431 (DC, 1/73); CGC NM+ 9.6, sold for $74 in 2013.

SUPERMAN, BATMAN REVAMPED

Superman also had some long-needed changes coming, beginning with *Superman* #233. In that issue, Clark Kent got a new job as a television journalist, but the big change would be with the one element deadly to the Man of Steel – kryptonite. Thanks to a "scientific experiment," all kryptonite on Earth turned to iron. Superman's powers would be scaled back as well, when the experiment had an unexpected side effect. After Superman was knocked back trying to stop a powerful explosion, his imprint in the sand opened a portal to another dimension, where a strange being escaped. It would become an exact duplicate of Superman, only composed entirely of sand, with the ability

to drain our hero's power into itself. Over the course of nine issues, Superman and his sand-doppelganger fought; by the end of the storyline, in issue #242, the Man of Steel had his powers reduced by 50 percent.

Batman, too, would make a few changes in the new decade, which saw Dick Grayson grow out of his role as Robin and move off to college. For the next few years, Batman would go it alone, as he had in his earliest adventures.

Superman's Pal Jimmy Olsen #133 (DC, 10/70); CGC NM/MT 9.8, sold for $806 in 2014. *The Forever People* #1 (DC, 2-3/71); Twin Cities pedigree, CGC NM/MT 9.8, sold for $1,673 in 2014. *The New Gods* #1 (DC, 2-3/71); CGC NM/MT 9.8, sold for $836 in 2013.

Mister Miracle #1 (DC, 3-4/71); CGC NM 9.4, sold for $262 in 2016. *Kamandi the Last Boy on Earth* #1 (DC, 10-11/72); CGC NM 9.4, sold for $89 in 2015. *The Demon* #1 (DC, 8-9/72); CGC NM 9.4, sold for $358 in 2017.

The biggest news from DC during this time was the return of Jack Kirby, who finally had left Marvel after several frustrating years. DC gave him free rein, beginning with a revamped *Superman's Pal Jimmy Olsen* series. Kirby introduced his "Fourth World" line-up, with *The Forever People, New Gods,* and *Mister Miracle,* and later with *Kamandi the Last Boy on Earth* and *The Demon.* In time, Jack returned to Marvel, but his presence at DC really stirred things up for a while.

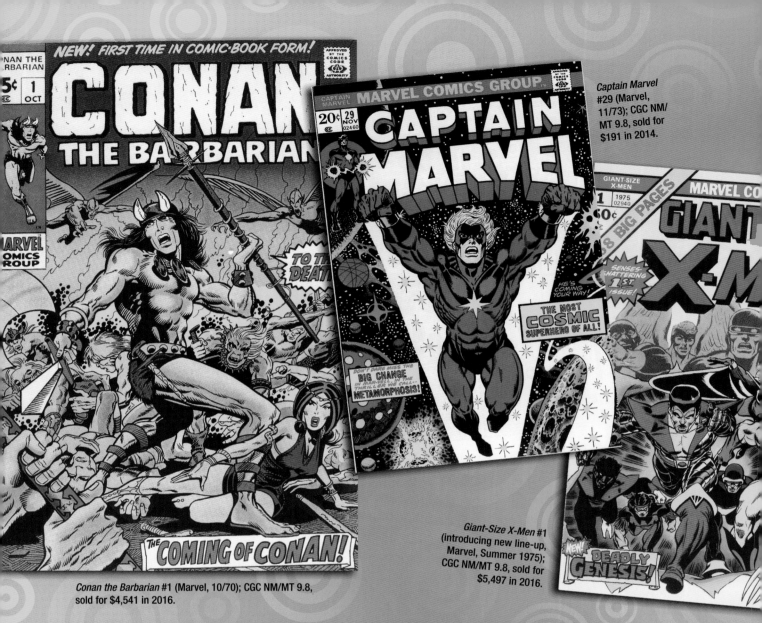

Captain Marvel #29 (Marvel, 11/73); CGC NM/ MT 9.8, sold for $191 in 2014.

Giant-Size X-Men #1 (introducing new line-up, Marvel, Summer 1975); CGC NM/MT 9.8, sold for $5,497 in 2016.

Conan the Barbarian #1 (Marvel, 10/70); CGC NM/MT 9.8, sold for $4,541 in 2016.

CONAN GIVES MARVEL A BOOST

Marvel would get a new lease on life when Roy Thomas and Barry Smith began their celebrated *Conan the Barbarian* series, which was inspired by Robert E. Howard's novels. The Conan stories had become popular as paperback editions sold throughout the sixties. There would also be big changes in store for Spider-Man, and especially for the X-Men, which was revamped in 1975 in a most successful way.

Artist/writer Jim Starlin shook things up with "cosmic" storylines for Captain Marvel and Warlock. Although he inherited both characters from previous creative teams, he left his own impression on the two; Warlock in particular was a fascinating, if somewhat convoluted, saga that stretched on for several issues; it was a cult

hit with many fans (including me – loved that "Cosmic Cube" device).

Another well-written (and lengthy) saga was writer Roy Thomas' "Kree-Skrull War" that ran in *The Avengers* issues #89-97 (June 1971 through March 1972). Neal Adams had a hand in illustrating a few issues, with brothers Sal and John Buscema also involved. Captain Marvel was prominently featured in this storyline, which also spotlighted the romance between Avengers Vision and Scarlet Witch. The entire series was eventually reprinted by Marvel as a trade paperback – it's worth seeking out.

Of course, this is only a small portion of the many great comic books issued during the 1970s, but further discussion on the subject will have to wait for another book!

FANDOM PROPELS THE HOBBY

Comics fandom would have an incredible impact on comic books. Thanks to the popularity of comic conventions, both young and old fans came together to meet the creators of their favorite titles, and hunt down back issues, going all the way back to the 1930s. Golden Age comic books were tough to find during the sixties (well, they were for me – I rarely saw anything older than late-fifties in used book stores). Now, they seemed to be readily available – for a price, of course. The first edition of Robert Overstreet's *Comic Book Price Guide* came out in 1970, legitimating serious comic book collecting. This was the big change that kept comic books on the stands, eventually resulting in the mass popularity for superheroes today.

It was finally true – comic books were not just for kids anymore!

Strange Tales #178 featuring Warlock (Marvel, 2/75); CGC NM+ 9.6, sold for $334 in 2016.

The Avengers #93 (Marvel, 12/71); CGC NM 9.4, sold for $537 in 2016.

▶ So it all comes down to this! Superman is finally forced to retire (it's naturally a "time travel" story, with the Man of Steel in the year 122,470) in *Action Comics* #386 (DC, 3/70). CGC graded NM+ 9.6, this sold for $119 in 2016.

COLLECTING SiLVER AGE SUPERHERO COMICS

PEOPLE COLLECT for all manner of reasons, but the number one reason is simple: a love of the subject. The same is true when it comes to comic books. It's true that investors have all but taken over the high-end collectible comics, but a certain love for them has to be present; otherwise, why not stick to stocks and bonds, or real estate for investment purposes?

On many of the graded and certified comics pictured in this book, you'll notice the name of a pedigreed collection. For these images, we have selected items from well-known pedigrees, such as the Boston, Don and Maggie Thompson, Pacific Coast, Savannah, and Twin Cities collections. Very few collections found today receive a pedigree designation; those that do are from truly exceptional groups of high-grade, well-preserved collections. Buying these books in today's marketplace can be incredibly expensive, and a hobby for collectors with very deep pockets.

But not all comic books certified in high grade are from pedigree collections, and not all collectors seek out only the highest-graded copies available. For many budget-minded collectors, mid-grade copies (Fine 6.0 to Very Fine 8.0) will do. A number of collectors don't want their vintage comics sealed up within a hard-plastic case, but prefer copies that can be read and enjoyed – usually those at Good 2.0 to Very Good 4.0 condition in a "raw" (uncertified) state are preferred. And for some key issues that can be cost-prohibited even in lower grades, "filler" copies in Fair 1.0 condition will suffice, until a better-condition copy can be afforded.

Vintage collectible comics are purchased by a variety of means. Some collectors form a relationship with one trusted dealer, and buy exclusively from that source, usually transacting their business by mail. Some collectors love "the thrill of the hunt" and prefer to track them down in yard sales, flea markets, and comic book conventions held in larger cities. Comic book stores can sometimes provide vintage material, along with recent releases, but shops tend to charge more – after all, they have an overhead to worry about. For high-end collectors, auction houses like Heritage are the best way to go. Auctions can attract buyers with budgets, as there are almost always a few bargains to be had at these events.

Gone are the days when comics were traded among kids who simply wanted to have fresh reading material, though. Even those youngsters starting their collections know that condition is important, and they handle their books with extreme care. It's really a different time from my heyday of collecting during the glorious Silver Age years, but it's the memory of buying new comics off the stands and swapping with like-minded friends that has kept me interested all these years. We loved to read the stories back then, and luckily for us "old-school" fans, the best of those old comics are available in reprint books that can withstand repeated reading.

Looking at old comic books is a lot of fun. Seems to me that's what got most of us hooked in the first place!

As Stan Lee would say, Excelsior, True Believers!

ACKNOWLEDGMENTS

i WOULD like to thank the following: Jim Halpern, Eric Bradley, Jim Lentz, Jim Steele, Barry Sandoval, and the Comics Staff at Heritage Auctions; Jeremy Shorr of Titan Comics; Richard Neal of Zeus Comics; Keith Colvin of Keith's Comics; Dave Mercer; Karen Wells; Mark Stokes; and a special thank you to my family, Sonia Tosh and Alexandra Welker.

Dedicated to the memory of my parents, Ross and Emma Tosh, for allowing me to read and keep all those comic books when I was young.

INDEX

A

B

C

D

O

P

Q

R

S

T

U

V

W

X

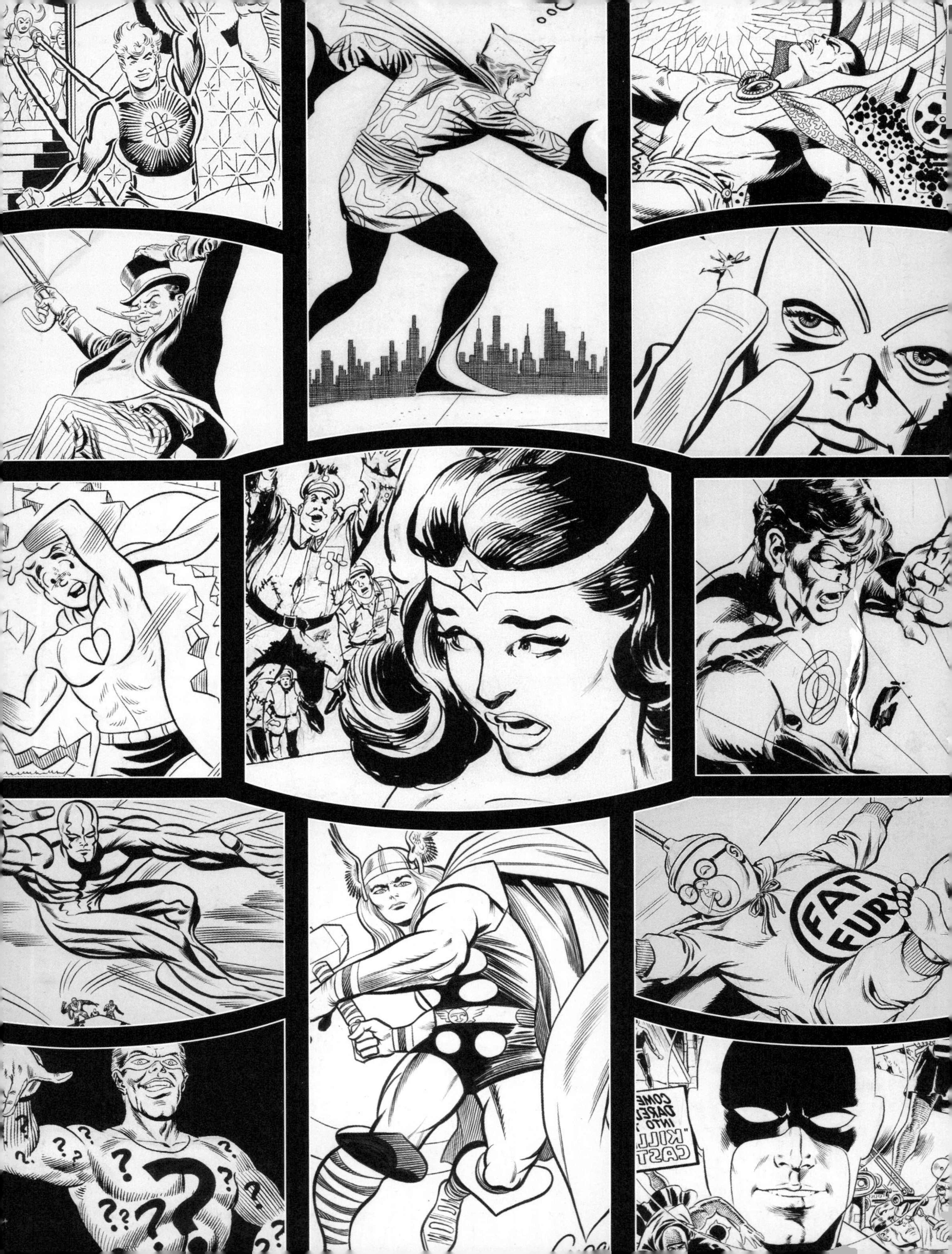
FAT
FURY